Anti-Tank

Anti-Tank

The Story of a Desert Gunner in the Second World War

Mark Carter

Northumberland County Council	
3 0132 02117370 8	
Askews & Holts	Jul-2012
940.548	£19.99

Pen & Sword
MILITARY

First published in Great Britain in 2012 by
Pen & Sword Military
47 Church Street
Barnsley
South Yorkshire
S70 2AS

ISBN 978 1 84884 811 5

A CIP catalogue record for this book is
available from the British Library.

Typeset in 11pt Palatino by Mac Style, Beverley, East Yorkshire
Printed and bound by the MPG Books Group Ltd.

Pen & Sword Books Ltd incorporates the Imprints of Pen & Sword
Aviation, Pen & Sword Family History, Pen & Sword Maritime, Pen
& Sword Military, Pen & Sword Discovery, Wharncliffe Local History,
Wharncliffe True Crime, Wharncliffe Transport, Pen & Sword Select,
Pen & Sword Military Classics, Leo Cooper, The Praetorian Press,
Remember When, Seaforth Publishing and Frontline Publishing.

For a complete list of Pen & Sword titles please contact
PEN & SWORD BOOKS LIMITED
47 Church Street, Barnsley, South Yorkshire, S70 2AS, England
E-mail: enquiries@pen-and-sword.co.uk
Website: www.pen-and-sword.co.uk

Contents

CHAPTER ONE

The big cross on that tank almost made me say a prayer, we were firing over open sights and the range was 200 yards. If we couldn't stop it it would run right over us. There were twenty tanks out there but as far as I was concerned there was only one. We got the rounds off faster than in any competition we'd had on the dummy loader back home, and we aimed for the tracks. Anything to stop that thing coming on. But we couldn't stop it. The gun swung round and the long shiny barrel came on to us. It was so close I could see the rifling inside. I could see our time running out there too.

It seemed only days since we had disembarked. After three months cooped up in a crowded troopship it was good to go ashore even if it was a fly-ridden dump like Egypt. However, the place had its compensation for it was in Cairo that I met Mary-Anne. She was Australian, a nursing sister from Tasmania. Australian girls are good to look at and this one was a dream. She had auburn hair with summer in her hazel eyes. She was the sort of girl you'd want to look at twice. She also had some nice perfume. I once made her tip a little on to my handkerchief for fear of spoiling a happy memory. We had a couple of precious weeks together and then goodbye Mary-Anne. We headed west with our guns into the 'blue'. That girl gave me something to think about. Somehow, I had never been able to get her out of my mind. I thought of her, then, as I tried to hit that tank…

It was March 1941. During the last couple of months the Italians had surrendered in droves. The coast road from Tobruk was crowded with fleeing troops, many of them still carrying their weapons and driving their own vehicles. Altogether ten divisions – over 200,000 men – surrendered. The British, who had captured huge quantities of loot, were beginning to think it wasn't such a bad war after all. Then reports came in that German units had been rushed to North Africa to help the Italians.

After days and nights of driving westward we came to a place called El Agheila which is west of Benghazi.

Rommel, the German commander, knew that the British army was weakened after sending troops to Greece. He knew, too, that our lines of communication stretched for hundreds of miles back into Egypt and that it would be difficult for us to bring up supplies of petrol and ammunition. Rommel, newly arrived in North Africa and acting under his own initiative, decided to strike hard for Benghazi and Tobruk. If he could smash his way through the British position before they had time to bring up reinforcements, all Egypt and the Suez Canal would lie within his grasp.

We stopped at El Agheila because we were exhausted and when we heard the sound of tank tracks we thought it was our own armour moving up ahead of us. It was then that this black-crossed monstrosity came grinding and rattling across the sand towards us. Our first German tank – and quite possibly our last…

We were firing HE (high explosive) because our supplies of armour piercing hadn't caught up with us. If only we could blow off its tracks. We got another round up the breech when I told my detachment to scatter. That tank was close. Unless we got out of the way we'd be rolled out flatter than my Aunt Sally's pastry mix!

As it turned out, that round was not wasted after all. The tank hit the gun and sent it ploughing across the desert. The gun snagged against a ledge of rock and the tank climbed over it. I just had time to see the gun crumple up like a piece of Meccano when that round went off. The tank was full of petrol and packed with ammunition and the explosion made me hard of hearing for weeks.

Number Two gun was blown over on to its side, the Sergeant and two of his men killed, the others wounded. The other tanks went right through our gun position and were heading for the wagon lines. We ran across and righted Number Two gun and, together with the remaining two guns of our troop, we got some shells off after them. Inevitably, some of those shells fell among our own men and when our medium guns opened up on us, mistaking us for Germans, I thought it was time we pulled out. However, before we could act, Palmer, our Battery Sergeant Major, strolled up. I don't think I ever saw him run. He was six foot four, a lean, serious type with a perpetual frown on his face. Always immaculately turned out he had earned himself the nickname of 'Starchy'. He stood looking about for our gun which seemed to have disappeared into thin air. Then he examined the smouldering remains of the tank and came on over to us.

In civilian life Palmer was a policeman. He wasn't very popular with our lot. I don't think he'd been very popular in the police either.

'Bit of a mess up here, Sergeant.'

He pointed to the tank tracks that led off across the desert. 'You had at least three hundred yards to play with.'

'We stopped that tank!'

I described what happened.

'You lost us a gun. You should get your eyes tested, Sergeant.'

'We had no armour piercing…'

The shells from the medium battery were churning up the sand in front of us but Palmer ignored them. He gave orders for the casualties to be removed.

'You and your crew take over Number Two gun,' he snapped. 'And get out of here before those medium bastards perform some kind of a miracle and get on to us.'

The trucks were racing up and we threw everything into them and when the guns were hooked up we drove off to a rendezvous with the rest of the battery in a wadi about two miles south of El Agheila.

The sun which that morning had risen blood red out of Egypt now stood high in the sky. The temperature was 120 degrees in the shade, only there wasn't any shade.

We spread out our camouflage netting and the guns were pulled round, facing westward. The Germans were expected at any moment. Men were trying to dig slit trenches but the ground was like concrete. Not only the gun detachments but cooks, batmen, office staff and even the officers worked stripped to the waist. All they wanted was to hack out a foot or two so that they could find some protection when the Germans started shelling. Despatch riders on their motorbikes weaved in and out among the vehicles. All engines were kept running and the combined exhaust fumes settled like a fog in the suffocating heat of the wadi.

The Battery Commander's truck. A group of sweating officers. A map spread out on the bonnet. The Battery Commander, Major 'Tubby' Wilson, had a fair complexion and his rather round face was burnt brick red by the sun. He pulled out his pistol and put it on the map as a paperweight. He addressed the troops standing round him.

'As you all know, the Germans have arrived and we have it on good authority that those tanks were part of their Fifth Light Division. They can't do much with one division but as you may have noticed they don't hang about. When they broke through us this morning they ran straight into the Eighth Medium who had a go over open sights. They knocked out some tanks but it was all too quick. The position now is that the bulk of that armour is way behind us and their supporting troops are following up. The Germans have already taken Benghazi and they're pushing on towards Tobruk. They'll be using the coast road so we'll just have to swing southwards and then go east across the desert the best way we can. No need for me to tell you we've got to reach Tobruk before they do.' He stopped to listen. It sounded as if somebody was tapping the bottom of a tin bath. We knew what it was and we wanted to duck. The first shell exploded about a hundred yards in front of us. Another shell threw up the sand behind us.

'Get out!' the Major yelled. 'The next lot'll drop right in here!'

It was not easy. We had already unloaded a lot of stuff including some shells and, when our truck came racing up, we tossed everything we could into the back, hooked up the gun and drove off into the desert. The Germans threw everything they had at that wadi. We could hear their stuff whistling overhead and all we could see back there was black rolling smoke.

In December 1940 Hitler believed that the huge well-equipped Italian army under Graziani would quickly push the British back into Egypt. He would then be willing to support them with aircraft and military supplies only, but he had no plans for a German army operation in such a distant and relatively unimportant place as North Africa. As far as he was concerned the big show was to be in Russia and in those early days nothing else seemed to matter. However, he was persuaded to order one division to proceed to North Africa as a morale booster for the Italians. When he heard that the Italians had collapsed and the British had taken Benghazi he was faced with the very real danger that the Allies would use North Africa as a springboard to invade southern Europe. He knew then that one division would not be enough and he ordered the 15th Panzer Division to be despatched to Tripoli with all speed.

Rommel's first objective was the strategically placed pass at Mersa el Brega. Here units of the British 2nd Armoured Division put up a desperate fight but Mersa el Brega fell and Rommel decided to keep going.

General Wavell, the British Commander, and his staff were taken completely by surprise. According to their information the Germans could not possibly be ready to attack. After all, they had only landed one Division. Then, as more alarming reports came in, a state of confusion ran through the British High Command. What kind of an army was this which, breaking all the rules of strategy, kept coming on across North Africa?

Rommel, using the same old Blitzkrieg technique that had been so successful in France and Belgium, sent out fast motorcycle reconnaissance patrols followed by tanks and motorized infantry. At Agedabia these troops raced through the British outposts before anyone had time to snatch up their weapons. For the Germans the onward sweep of their advance was exhilarating. Benghazi with all its stores and port installations fell virtually intact. Then on to Derna and Tobruk. Soon they would be racing along the coast road towards Alexandria.

But the lorries loaded with stores and heavy equipment, the trucks which pulled the guns across the endless desert roads and, most of all, the tanks soon ran out of petrol and came to a halt. Rommel, in a top priority operation, had petrol rushed to them from the west and, before the British could exploit the position, their advance continued.

Meanwhile the British blew up their own underground fuel supplies to deny its use by the enemy. This was a big mistake because units of the 7th Armoured Division which were pressing forward to engage the enemy were unable to refuel.

Two British generals were captured and the British fell back in confusion while the Egyptians got ready to hang out their Nazi flags.

We gathered scraps of information from the scattered bands of fleeing troops. The news was always the same: strong German forces approaching Tobruk. Going eastward made me cling to some faint hope. Who knows, maybe one day we'd end up back in Cairo.

The desert was flat and stony, the visibility restricted because of the heat shimmer. And we lost that most popular of vehicles, the water wagon. Our water was rationed so we had to choose between drinking the warm brackish stuff or washing and shaving with it. Sometimes we would do both and then wash our feet with the dregs. It was the same with tea. Often we left a little in the bottom of our mugs to shave with. We all hated the desert. The pitiless glare, the harsh tableland of yellow sand can have a depressing effect on a man. He longs for the night when the stars are friendly and the desert has sunk into blackness, merciful oblivion.

We passed through the old Italian border defences with Egypt. Miles of twisted and broken barbed wire, old trenches and ruined pillboxes. There were many graves here. Men were not just buried in the desert. Heavy stones had to be found and put together on top of the grave to prevent the jackals getting at the bodies. There were old minefields here and the engineers laid some tapes and we held our breath as we made our way between these rudimentary guidelines.

I'd been doing a spell of driving when I saw Mary-Anne. It was her eyes I think that made me swerve – deep and cool and serene. She smiled at me and then she vanished. Hours of driving? An exhausted mind? Hallucinations? Maybe, but that was the best mirage I had ever seen. I was thirsty and I would have gone without water all day just to get another glimpse of her.

We drove all that day and into the night. The following day we caught up with what was left of our Division. The radio reports were shattering. Tobruk was still holding out and the Germans, rather than enter into a long siege, had by-passed the town. Then, when we heard Bardia had fallen, it seemed that all that stood between the German army and the whole of Egypt were our three guns.

News of the newly arrived 15th Panzer Division came without warning in the shape of ranging shots from a battery of 88mm guns. Originally designed as an anti-aircraft weapon the 88mm was used as a field gun with devastating effect.

The tannoy blared. The GPO's voice: 'Take post!' Then came the range followed by the angle to be put on the gun. Those 88mm shells were getting too close for comfort. Our only cover was the gun and we could hardly lie down behind that. Since we had lost Number One gun and taken over Number Two we automatically became

One again. I mention this because Number One gun is usually the ranging gun and prides itself on having the best detachment.

My crew were a pretty mixed lot. There was Rod Wainwright, my number two, tall and thin, a serious type. Joe Banks, a lanky ex-miner from Yorkshire. He joined up after a bet with some friends. He got himself so drunk he hadn't realized what he was doing. Thomas Rule from Pontypridd was also a miner. Short and thin with a long face, he'd also been an ardent Salvation Army man in the valleys where he worked. If he didn't talk about ponies down the pit it was religion. Johnny Corbett was a big tough Geordie with a face like a prizefighter and he'd worked in the docks at Tyneside. He was a loud-mouthed argumentative type who liked to drink and pick fights. Then there was Doug Walton, thin and bony with sunken cheeks and gloomy eyes. He was a grave digger in a big London cemetery. That vocation, at least, would come in handy out here. Lastly myself, 'Sarge' as they called me. I'd been looking for adventure. The war was looming. I joined the Royal Horse Artillery.

I suppose you could say that I found my adventure although it was a little too high for me sometimes. And there we were, about to take on an 88mm. It was rather like a destroyer trying to take on a battleship. I soon found myself wondering why those 88s couldn't stick to their anti-aircraft role and leave us poor field gunners in peace.

We kept them busy for a while but if we hadn't had a good OP officer – he'd taken up a position behind a sandhill only 500 yards from their guns – they would have blasted us off the desert. Then they started putting up airbursts. These were shells which exploded twenty to thirty feet above the ground and sent jagged shards of steel splaying over a wide area of the ground below. Airbursts were a lethal nightmare. We fired so many rounds that our barrel became very hot and we had no water to spare for cooling it.

Later, when some tanks were spotted, we pulled out and for the next few days we were constantly on the move, in and out of action, shooting up guns, tanks and motorized infantry. They were long hot days of forced marches with hardly any food or water. Sometimes a sandstorm would force us to halt and we would grope about in the choking yellow murk. Sandstorms were sometimes so fierce they could take the paint off a vehicle.

One day we put our camouflage netting up outside a place called Capuzzo. We were too tired to dig slit trenches. We brewed some tea, opened up a few tins of bully beef and spent an uneasy night. From the west we could hear the churning of engines and there was a constant flickering in the sky like summer lightning and always that steady rumble of gunfire. Somewhere over there an army was on the move, coming our way, hell bent to blast their way through into Egypt. We heard Tobruk was still holding out and naval units helped to keep the garrison going by creeping in at night with supplies and reinforcements. The Germans were determined to take Tobruk because it tied up a considerable number of their troops and held up their main advance eastward. Then, when we heard reports that German tanks were coming along the coast road towards Sollum I knew, somehow, that Cairo was as far away as ever.

I found myself sitting next to Doug Walton and we chatted.

'Whatever made you go in for grave digging?'

Walton was tired of being asked this question and he was also more fed up than usual. 'The money's good, besides, there are some good perks.'

'Perks?'

'People like to be buried with rings and things. You know, sentimental folk and such.'

I shifted uneasily. Had I got a ghoul in my gun crew? 'You wouldn't touch anything...'

'They're not going to need them any more.'

I wondered whether he was pulling my leg but he appeared to be serious. 'The best pickings can be found in the old family vaults.'

He seemed pleased to be able to get a dig in at me. I found his conversation disturbing and I wondered whether he would take some things off me when my turn came. I broke a long silence. 'Those old vaults must get pretty crowded. How on earth do you fit the new arrivals in?'

'Oh I take a broom in there with me. Mind you, you have to watch out if you want a fag. Strike a match and as likely as not you'd be blown sky high!'

'What are you talking about?'

'Gas of course. Dead bodies can give off an explosive mixture more powerful than the stuff we use to bang a shell off at the bloody Germans.'

I wanted to change the subject but I was so tired I couldn't think of anything to say.

'Come to think of it,' Walton said, 'the supply must be endless. If the folk at home ever run out of gas they could pipe that stuff straight to their kitchens.'

Rod Wainwright got up to fill his can with tea and I went across to join him.

'The Germans didn't lose much time getting here. All they've got is one Division,' I said. 'With these huge distances and petrol to worry about they'll soon fizzle out.'

All the same, the arrival of the Germans in North Africa was disturbing. They had the mightiest army the world had ever seen. They had conquered most of Europe. They had only to cross that narrow part of the Mediterranean between Sicily and Tripoli in sufficient numbers to push us all right out of Egypt.

At this moment we were alone. Neither America nor Russia had entered the war. It looked as if the British desert army was about to take on the whole might of the German Wehrmacht.

'I stopped by the radio truck today,' Rod said. 'The Germans have got plenty of petrol. There are rushing up another Division too. And if they do capture Tobruk they can bring all their supplies ashore there.'

'The Aussies are in Tobruk, the Guards too. They'll take some shifting.'

'I heard they were by-passing the place. Looks like they're hell bent for Egypt and the Suez Canal.'

I began to feel depressed. This, obviously, was what it was all about.

'Not to mention the Persian oilfields,' I reminded him.

I tried to picture the Germans in Cairo. The Nazi flags would be hanging out everywhere. They would take over Shepheards and probably make it their headquarters. Farouk would either collaborate with them or disappear down the Red Sea in his yacht. And Mary-Anne? My stomach gave a lurch.

'The Gypos wouldn't know what hit them if the Germans arrived,' Rod said. 'Come to think of it, it might be a good idea. The Germans would soon clean up that dump and if the Gypos didn't behave they'd probably let the Med in and drown the lot.'

I don't think anybody liked the Egyptians. They didn't lift a finger when the Italians invaded their country. They let the British do all the dirty work and as long as they could go on with their wheeling and dealing they were content to shelter beneath the umbrella of the British Army. Not that they could have put up a fight anyway and they were always ready to come in on the winning side. As for Cairo, the street traders, especially, were a menace. They would follow you for miles and drive you crazy with their pestering. They would take your last penny and cut your throat into the bargain if they had the chance. Much as I relished the thought of the Germans in Cairo I would have been worried about Mary-Anne. I knew that if anything like that happened I would never see her again.

'Remember the Tipperary Club?' Rod asked me.

The Tipperary Club. Run mainly by British and Commonwealth women and home from home for the ordinary soldier, it was just round the corner from Shepheards. Here you could leave the hot crowded smelly streets and almost find yourself back in the cool peace of an English café. Many of the soldiers who crowded into the Tipperary Club came straight from the desert. Here they could drink tea or have a decent meal and scribble their letters home.

'I met a smashing girl last time I was in Cairo,' Rod said. 'A nurse she was. Australian. She works at the hospital there.'

It couldn't be, and yet, for the troops, Cairo was a small world.

'What sort of nurse?' I tried to be calm.

Rod stared at me. 'What do you mean, what sort? There's only one kind. Slim, very dark and with the bluest of eyes.'

I discovered that I could breathe again. 'Join the club. I met my girl in Cairo. She's Australian and she works at the hospital too.'

It was Rod's turn to look uneasy. 'Don't worry, she's fair,' I grinned, 'and her eyes are hazel.'

I told him about Mary-Anne.

Rod passed me a snapshot of his girlfriend. It had been taken with the Sphinx and a pyramid in the background.

'Her name's Kate,' he said. 'Kate McDonald.'

I must admit she was very pretty and it struck me then that I had no picture of Mary-Anne – not even a street photographer's snap.

'Sometimes when things are crazy up here I tell myself I'm fighting the Germans just to keep them away from her.'

'That's a good enough reason,' Rod said. 'One thing's for sure, I'm not going back to England without Kate.'

'She might want you to go to Australia with her.'

Rod grinned. 'Then I'll go to Australia. What about you?'

'Mary-Anne? I'd marry her tomorrow if I could get this war out of the way.'

During their advance eastwards the Germans took Halfaya Pass, a desolate boulder-strewn area of ravines and dried-up river beds. Here, the main coast road wound its way up an escarpment to the plateau east of Sollum. Halfaya Pass was a strategic position and the British would have to re-take it if they wanted to push Rommel back and relieve Tobruk.

In May the British attacked and threw the Germans out of the pass but Rommel was determined to recapture it. If he could hold the pass he could prevent the British from using Sollum – a short distance along the road – to bring in supplies and reinforcements.

Towards the end of May the Germans attacked, swinging round through the desert to take the British in the rear. Their motorized infantry and assault groups attacked the pass from two sides. Their shells streamed into the wadis and ravines, bursting among the rocks and inflicting heavy casualties on the British defenders. Then, after bitter hand-to-hand fighting, they re-took the pass.

We had been in action in the desert south of Halfaya and now we headed north and set our guns down in a shallow valley at the eastern end of the pass itself. We were soon to take part in the big offensive, Operation BATTLEAXE, which was planned to push the Germans out of the pass for good.

Other strongpoints such as Point 208, which was deep in the desert, would also be attacked. The British would then move westward across the desert and relieve Tobruk.

Once, when the desert was fairly quiet, a replacement gun was delivered to us to make the strength of our troop up to four guns again. The Observation Post Officer also paid us a visit. His assistant had been killed and because I had done some specialist work he wanted me to give him a hand for a day or two.

The OP is often situated well forward where the fall of shot can be seen and necessary corrections sent back to the guns, most of us Sergeants had been up to the OP before, of course, but I think we were all glad to get back. An OP can be a pretty hot spot and you were inclined to feel vulnerable stuck out there on your own.

The Germans had their OPs too and often when their shells were dropping close we had the feeling we were being watched.

Captain Jackson, the OP officer, was a fair-haired serious ex-schoolmaster and, even out there, something of that vocation still clung to him for he would sometimes bring out a blackboard easel and a piece of chalk when he lectured us about gunnery.

'You Sergeants hang around the guns too much,' he told me. 'When things are quiet you should take the opportunity to get away for a few hours and see how the other half lives. This will be a chance to polish up on your specialist work. After all, if you want to be an officer one day you've got to know something about OP work.'

Frankly I had no desire to become an officer – not for some time at any rate. I was perfectly happy – if that's the right word – to remain with my crew. They were a rough lot but when you've been in action and seen some hard times together you tend to get set in your ways. We were Number One gun, too, which was quite something. Maybe if the war dragged on I'd apply for a commission but if I went back to Cairo for the training I'd miss all my friends and I'd be sure to be posted to a different unit afterwards.

On the following day, soon after first light, Jackson and I started out on our journey to the OP and we followed the telephone line which Jackson and his assistant had laid down a few days previously. It was a long rough scramble. We climbed over some big boulders and pushed our way through the thorn bushes all the way to the top. We were rewarded with a wonderful view of the desert, though, and that sunrise made me wish I'd brought a camera.

The OP was just a pile of stones put together to form a crude shelter and it lay high up on the boulder- strewn slopes close to a shrine of the Madonna that the Italians had put up there. Below us, the pass – wide, deep and gloomy – wound its way through a wilderness of crags and ravines until it reached the approaches to Sollum in the west. We could see for miles although any sense of distance was swallowed up in the vastness of the landscape.

'Look!' Jackson pointed.

The sun, beginning to dip into the pass, glinted on the barrel of a gun. The Germans hadn't bothered to put up any camouflage netting and we could see the dark squat shapes of tanks crowded up against the overhanging cliffs. Jackson handed me his glasses and the pass sprang to life. I could see men unloading wagons, putting up barbed wire and building sandbag walls round the gun emplacements and machine-gun nests.

We kept very still, trying not to dislodge any stones, and once when I looked round I could have sworn somebody came up behind us, but it was only the long shadow of the Madonna. The Italians did a good job and I was struck by her tranquil beauty. I felt that I was an intruder, a violator of the peace of this sanctuary.

Jackson caught me looking at her and he nodded. 'There's been some shelling up here. Strange but there's not a chip on that Madonna!'

Almost as if the Germans had heard the remark there was a puff of smoke and Jackson pulled me down. The shell burst about fifty yards in front of us and showered us with dirt and stones.

'Fifty yards short. Now if they were to raise the elevation slightly you and I could sit down to tea with that Madonna.'

'Speak for yourself.' I knew who I was more likely to have tea with.

The next shell sent steel splinters and chips of rock like driven hail across the OP. It was scary. Being shelled in the desert was bad enough. Up here on the mountain slopes you were just as likely to be struck by the whizzing rocks as the fragments of steel.

'It's an eighty-eight!' Jackson shouted. He rang down figures to the guns.

'Range four thousand. Number One gun fire when ready.'

Number One gun. And here I was stuck up here like a fish out of water. I listened for the gun to fire but the 88 shells were making too much of a racket. Without me would they get anywhere near the target? When I saw that first burst of smoke and heard the echoing crump of the shell which fell only about a hundred yards short I realized nobody was indispensable.

'Range four thousand two hundred. Fire!'

This time I heard a distinct slam as the gun fired. A pause, then the shell whistled through the gorge and burst about a hundred yards ahead of the 88. It was a nice bracket.

'Range four thousand one hundred. Ten rounds gunfire. Fire!'

Next minute each of our four guns blasted off ten rounds and forty shells fell around the 88 and silenced it.

'It's not just the angle and range you've got to work out,' Jackson said, 'you've got to allow for the weight of the projectile and the muzzle velocity of the gun.

Then there's wind and drift to take into account.'

He went into a long discourse on the science of ballistics and I am sure that if his blackboard and easel had been there he'd have found a piece of chalk and gone to work. We spent all day up there plotting targets and sending the information down to our guns.

In the desert there is hardly any dusk. The sun disappears and darkness descends quickly. In the Pass the process is accelerated and the night can be black as pitch. When it suddenly grew dark Jackson said 'We've left it a bit late to start back now. We'd never make it in the dark and we can't use a torch. Besides, the Germans send out night patrols. Imagine what they'd do if they clobbered us and captured our OP.'

I shall never forget that night. The little cooking fires that sprang up from the German positions, the shouting and the singing and the laughter that floated up to us. It didn't seem to bother them that it gave their positions away. Certainly Jackson hadn't the heart to call fire down on them. They didn't fire on us either. For some reason – unlike the open desert where the guns would blast away night and day – there seemed to be an unwritten law, a policy of live and let live in that pass at night.

It was hot. There was not a breath of wind and their songs came up to us. Marching songs. 'Lili Marlene.' They even sang 'Tipperary'. Jackson brought out some whisky and we sang too.

Imagination, or was that a cheer which floated up from the bottom of the pass? We finished the whisky and started on another bottle.

We took turns to sleep and we both stood to at dawn. The colours in that sky took my breath away. How could so much beauty herald in another day of killing? The telephone rang. A change in plan. Operation BATTLEAXE was to take place that morning and there was only ten minutes to go! Jackson uncorked his water bottle and tipped the water over his head, rubbing his face as the water ran over him.

'Operation BATTLEAXE and not a word of warning. I'm afraid you're stuck with me up here, Sergeant.'

For a schoolmaster he could swear. 'No time even for a cup of tea….

Jackson went to work like a man possessed. He plotted the enemy targets and worked out the angles and the range and telephoned the information and other technical data down to the guns. When somebody on the other end of the line complained that he should have had the information earlier Jackson was furious.

'If you think you can do any better then come on up here. Ten minutes. How the hell did I know you were going to shove BATTLEAXE down my neck this morning?'

While he spat out the figures I became increasingly uneasy. If it was going to be something big I wanted to be with my own gun team.

'Shut up, Sergeant!' His face was lined with fatigue and he looked as if he hadn't shaved for days.

'If you want a job then check the weapons. Once this thing starts we're going to need them!'

I knew what he meant. In a big attack the Germans would go all out to knock out our OP. After all, we had been doing them quite a lot of damage already.

Jackson had brought a Bren gun up with him while I had my rifle. We had also lugged a box of grenades up there and I took out a dozen and put them in a handy place. Jackson slammed the telephone down and came across to me.

'One minute to go. Oh, by the way, you'd better get your bayonet fixed!'

That startled me. Was I supposed to make some sort of last ditch stand up here – fixed bayonet and all?

He saw my hesitation. 'What do you think it's for?'

I felt a bit of an idiot as I yanked out my bayonet, particularly as the point was stained with a reddish-brown from opening bully beef tins. After all, I was no infantryman of the line. I was a Sergeant in the Royal Horse Artillery. A nineteen thirty-niner and a volunteer at that.

Jackson pulled out his revolver and examined the chamber. Then he picked up the Bren gun and slung it across his shoulder. I began to feel even more uncomfortable. I'd had my eye on that weapon and I thought Jackson would let me use it. A Bren gun was something. A rifle was pretty useless. A bayonet…I shivered. It was chilly up there in the early morning.

The barrage opened with a crash which tore the sky apart and a rushing sound like wild geese winging their way across the pass made us get our heads down. The din of the artillery rose to a massive drumming which shook the hill and loosened the stones of our crude shelter. All we could see below us was a thick blanket of smoke. I knew that if BATTLEAXE was successful our troops would advance and we would both get out of there. But the bombardment went on for hours while Jackson continued to pass corrections down to the guns. Then, when the barrage lifted, and the guns started to search out targets which lay deeper in the pass, the Germans decided that it was time they knocked out our OP.

Two truck-loads of infantry came racing up to the foot of the hill and steel helmeted figures jumped down and started to scramble up the boulder-strewn slopes. Being on a twenty-five pounder field gun is different. I had never shot at a man with a rifle before and I still don't know whether I would have pressed the trigger if they hadn't opened up first and blasted that hillside. Anyway, compared with the stuff they were sending up at us I might as well have tried to answer them with an air gun. The magazine held five rounds and that barely lasted me five seconds and by the time I had reloaded the Germans were halfway up the hill. Jackson, who was still on the telephone, practically threw the Bren gun at me.

'Here, see what you can do with this!'

I knew the Bren gun inside out and I could take the thing down and put it together again in minutes. It was a good machine gun and I liked the feel of it. I had fired it back on the ranges but I never dreamed I would need it for the real thing. You were supposed to set it up on a tripod or fire it lying down while using its two front legs as a support. Jackson had not brought the tripod with him and the ground was too rocky for me to use it lying down. I held it like a Tommy gun and fired a burst but the weapon kicked back and the shots went wild. In the end I managed to prop the barrel up against a ledge of rock.

I cursed Jackson because I wanted him to give me a hand but he was still glued to the telephone. We could, of course, bring fire down on the Germans from our own Battery, but we would probably get hit too, and if I got myself killed by Number One gun, for instance, my crew would never stop scoffing about it.

Bren-gun ammunition is heavy stuff to cart around and I quickly used up the few magazines we'd brought with us. I was back with my rifle and bayonet.

The Germans, under cover of some rocks called on us to surrender but somehow I couldn't imagine Jackson producing a white flag – not that we had anything white with us anyway. Another truck raced up, more troops jumped down and then they started to unload a mortar. A red flare burst overhead and the assault force came out from under their cover and moved forward. When Jackson tore off his earphones and brought out his revolver I knew I wasn't going to use my bayonet for opening bully beef tins.

I remembered the grenades. I'd seen what an 88 shell can do but by the time we used up those grenades this was a close second. The grenades, bursting among the flint-like rocks and stones, turned that hillside into a butcher's shop.

Then, above the din, we heard the clank and squeal of tank tracks – that jangle of tortured metal which seems to scream out for oil. Were the Germans so desperate they needed to call up tanks to deal with two men? The crash of gunfire from our own lines reminded us that Operation BATTLEAXE was well under way and we could see our own shells bursting among the German positions farther up the pass. Below us a great cloud of yellow dust spread out across the pass and we heard the whining of engines. Next minute we saw those tanks.

They were our own Mark IIs, the very latest for speed, weaponry and armour. All part of a big shipment, together with crews, rushed to North Africa. The German assault group retreated back down the hill and I glanced up at the Madonna. Imagination, or was that the faintest of smiles?

The Germans had brought several 88s into Halfaya Pass and concealed them in stone emplacements which merged into the landscape and were practically invisible. As the leading tank drove forward one of these guns fired and the turret flew off. Another shell blew off its tracks. The following tank managed to push it off the road and keep going but an armour-piercing shell smashed into it, the ammunition exploded and the tank became an inferno. Jackson and I waited for the crew to bale out but nothing happened. The hatch had probably jammed with the heat.

The pass echoed and re-echoed to the crash of gunfire. The dust cloud became a fog. Then came the roar of engines. There must have been fifty of our tanks down there. Behind them came the infantry, tight knots of men, hurrying to keep up, trying to get what protection they could from the steel monsters in front of them.

Then the 88s again. A scream of high-velocity shells and one tank and then another received direct hits and burst into flames. We watched the crews bale out only to be cut down by the vicious German crossfire on either side of the valley. One of the tanks ran into a minefield and a mine blew off its tracks. The crew spilled out and tried to escape but they were blown to pieces on the minefield. They might have been better off if they'd stayed inside their tank.

This was no battle of tank against tank. There was not a single enemy tank in sight. The Germans were keeping their armour for use in the open desert where they could manoeuvre properly. What in fact we were witnessing was nothing less than a proving ground for the German 88mm all-purpose gun. The British Mark II tank, upon which everybody had pinned their hopes, had met more than its match.

Soon the floor of the pass became littered with blazing hulks and the infantry, caught in the open, were either blown up in the minefield or cut down by machine-gun fire. Out of the fifty tanks only twelve turned round and got out of there. Halfaya Pass on that first day of Operation BATTLEAXE became a tank graveyard. Jackson rang through to the Command Post but the line was dead. The Germans started to shell us again and we decided it was time to get out. As we scrambled down the mountainside and hurried past the burning tanks I knew why Halfaya Pass had earned the name Hellfire Pass from the soldiers of the Desert Army. I knew, too, that for all of us it was going to be a long and bloody summer.

CHAPTER TWO

Smoke stood over Sollum. The town, bombed, shelled and burning was in its death throes. The Germans were pulling out to avoid being cut off by the advancing British who by-passed Halfaya Pass and were pushing westward. However, soon they would be reinforced by the newly-arrived 15th Panzer Division, so we all knew that our attack was not going to be a walk-over.

The first phase of Operation BATTLEAXE was to take Halfaya Pass and Point 208. The success of the entire plan of attack depended on removing these two threats from our rear. However, these key German positions held out.

Originally a fortification set up by the Italians deep in the desert south east of Bardia, Point 208 was the pivot of the German forces in that area. The Germans built a fortified system of trenches, sandbagged enclosures and pillboxes there. Point 208 could boast of a little shade and a well of barely drinkable water – and the 88mm gun.

A British armoured brigade approached Point 208 with about seventy Mark II tanks and infantry carriers. The Germans held their fire until they were almost on top of them. Then at point-blank range the 88 shells smashed into them while the infantry, caught in the open, came under a hail of fire and simply withered away. Here, as in Halfaya Pass, the British lost most of their tanks. Again the 88mm all-purpose gun was bad news.

We drove westward, a long column of guns, tanks and lorries. The desert was flat, burnt-out, blasted – like some dead planet scorched by a pitiless sun. We longed for the night although even then the desert gave off a heat which made you sweat.

The column halted, jam-packed, on the road but nobody knew what the hold up was about. A despatch rider came roaring up, weaving in and out among the vehicles and, looking back, I could see the General's caravan, an immense vehicle fitted out with lounge chair, sofa, table and almost every useful commodity that could be brought into the desert on wheels.

The Battery Commander, 'Tubby' Wilson, stood up in his truck and studied the front of the column with his glasses. Hardly anyone strayed off the road for fear of mines but the despatch rider, throwing caution to the wind, came racing back along the verge.

We had just got a nice brew-up going when three planes came screaming out of the sky. Stukas! It was said that the Germans fitted special sirens to the wings of these planes. Whatever it was, that nerve-rending sound will stay with me for ever. Explosions, fountains of sand, black smoke. Men and pieces of smashed vehicles were blown into the air. A wheel complete with axle hurtled past our truck and buried itself in the sand. An office truck was hit, sending files, typewriters and reams of paper into the air. Tins, pieces of equipment and dismembered bodies rained on to the desert. The planes wheeled and came back, very low, machine guns blazing. Wilson was yelling at us to fire with rifles, Bren guns or anything else. One man, almost beside himself with excitement, tossed up a hand grenade. Unfortunately, he misjudged the weight of the missile, and the grenade burst above his head and riddled him with steel splinters.

The planes vanished, leaving a smoking trail of chaos. Men staggered about blindly. Infantrymen and engineers, tank crews, cookhouse and the office staff were all mixed up together. Others lay dead or dying by their trucks. I heard the cry for stretcher bearers but I couldn't see any. I think their transport, too, was blasted. I couldn't see what had happened to the General's caravan because of the smoke. Tubby Wilson ordered us to manhandle our guns off the road.

'We've got to get the guns clear in case they come back. And we're needed up there. The Germans are all over the place!'

We hooked the guns up to whatever trucks were still serviceable and, risking the mines, we left the shattered convoy and headed west across the desert. Direction: the front.

We came up against advanced units of the 15th Panzer Division south of Bardia and went into action against tanks at an opening range of 3,000 yards. We hoped that a few rounds of gunfire would shift them but they turned suddenly and came straight towards us. The tannoy blared:

'Tanks, gunfire, gun control!'

That order ripped into us because now we knew that we were alone. We were independent of the rest of the Battery, and we would have to engage those tanks over open sights. I counted thirty tanks out there. German Mark IIIs and IVs Tanks with 75mm guns and superior to our own. They seemed to wobble about in the heat like jellies as they came towards us.

'Range two thousand. Fire!'

The gun leapt in a cloud of dust. Corbett yanked open the breech and smoke poured out as Walton thrust in another round. The breech slammed shut with a clang.

'Fire!'

The gun leapt again. Shouts, orders, corrections.

'Fire!'

The breech clanged with the monstrous regularity of a funeral bell. There was a heavy stink of cordite and the gun kicked up so much dust that with the smoke it was sometimes difficult to see the target. The Battery Commander radioed for support but our tanks – which should have been out there – were still sitting back on the road, smoking burnt-out hulks.

The leading tank was about 200 yards away when I noticed that some of our armour-piercing shells were bouncing off or becoming embedded in the steel casing. Then a lucky shot found the ammunition and the tank blew up. The turret flew through the air like a meteor and plunged into the desert behind us. There was so much smoke we couldn't see the following tank until it was very close. We fired point-blank and blew off one of its tracks. The tank slewed about crazily and presented its side to us. The gun swung round on to us but the crew held their fire because another tank suddenly roared up and crossed in front of it.

For some reason hand grenades had been in short supply during Operation BATTLEAXE – probably because most of them went to the infantry. Doug Walton, our grave digger, however, devised a simple and effective alternative against tanks. Before the action started he filled about a dozen bottles with petrol and tied some oily cotton waste round the top of each bottle. The trick was to light the rag and toss the bottle on top of a tank. It was then hoped that the burning liquid would run down the air holes and apertures into the control cabin and ignite the oil and grease that often lies like a film in the hot interior of a tank. A lucky throw might send the liquid fire running down into the engine itself, or the flames might even reach the ammunition.

Doug Walton tied four of these bottles – or Molotov Cocktails as they later became known – together with string for greater effect. The tank we'd disabled was swivelling round on its one track as it tried to get its gun to bear on us again. Doug grabbed his set of bottles and started to fumble about with some matches but they were wet with the sweat that soaked his clothes. The bullets were whistling about him as he brought out his lighter. He lit the four oily bits of cotton waste and then he ran up close to the tank and tossed the bottles on to the roof. There was a tinkle of broken glass and the petrol exploded with a roar. The flaming liquid ran down the ventilation shafts and the tank started to belch smoke from a dozen different places. The hatch opened and the crew scrambled out, their clothing on fire.

Our main concern now was to get clear before the tank blew up. However, we did stop to pull our gun well clear. We probably owe our lives to that German tank crew for not only did they block the following tank with their own burning hulk, they staggered about blindly while trying to put out their burning clothes.

The grave digger was fumbling about with his lighter but before he could get another bottle going the tanks were past us. A tank will hardly ever turn round and come back. Once it has broken through an enemy line it tends to get the bit between its teeth and keep going. Maybe it's something to do with the old cavalry days. Anyway, it was their bad luck, because there we were still with our guns and able to knock hell out of them another day.

When we came up against the 15th Panzer Division we little knew that Rommel had withdrawn the 5th Light Division from that same area and despatched it to Point 208 with instructions to press on eastward to Sidi Omar and Sidi Suleman to try and get behind the British and outflank them. At the same time he withdrew his forces from the Capuzzo front and sent them to join the 5th Light Division. This was a bold and clever move because the British forces

– advancing westward – now stood in danger of being cut off from the rear.

The front collapsed and we joined the long columns of retreating troops that streamed back eastwards across the desert. The Germans still held Halfaya Pass and their wide sweep south-eastwards was aimed at linking up with these troops. The British slipped through their net and made a stand east of the pass but they were as far away as ever from the garrison in Tobruk.

Operation BATTLEAXE failed largely because of the superiority of the German 88mm gun and, also, because we could not take out that vital enemy pivot, Point 208, or capture Halfaya Pass.

The Germans were in no condition to follow up their successes. Their line of communication from Tripoli, some 1,000 miles away, was too far for them to bring up the much needed supplies of petrol and ammunition in time. They also had to contend with Tobruk, that perpetual thorn in their side.

We pulled out of the line at the end of June because our gun barrels were worn out and also many of our wagons had been shot up and damaged by aircraft. This was a time when almost every plane you saw in the sky was a German, and if a British plane flew overhead it would be the signal for derisive cheering. Maybe it was something to do with the situation at home but our troops in North Africa began to feel bitter at the lack of support from the Desert Air Force at this time.

It was typical of life in the desert that news of leave came suddenly. I was one of the lucky ones and so were Johnny Corbett and Thomas Rule. The others could go when we got back. We had ten whole days and the truck was leaving for Cairo in fifteen minutes. We had no time to wash and shave or find clean clothes. I grabbed my pack and was ready to go.

I could hardly believe my luck. During the last few weeks I'd practically forgotten about Mary-Anne and now, suddenly, I realized I would see her again. Then, after about fifty miles of bumping about in clouds of dust, tired and thirsty, a kind of reaction set in and I began to wonder whether I should forget the whole thing and not bother to see her after all. I could have a few drinks, relax and save myself a lot of trouble. Besides, with all those troops in Cairo she'd probably forgotten me anyway. I was a front-line soldier, I reminded myself. Here today and maybe gone tomorrow! With me a girl was all or nothing and it would not be fair for either of us if we were to start up a close relationship. Then, when I brought out my handkerchief – the one she'd tipped that perfume on to – I changed my mind.

'What are you going to do in Cairo?' I asked Corbett.

'What do you think? Steak egg and chips and for afters I'll go along to the Birka.'

Rule, the Salvation Army man, was shocked. That Johnny Corbett, a married man who had been so close to death all this time, should now want to spend what might well be his last days on earth with a prostitute was beyond him.

'You're crazy. You might as well jump into the Sweetwater!'

The Sweetwater Canal in Egypt. We were warned that if anybody fell into it they would have to have a massive course of injections.

'Can you suggest a better way to spend my time?' Corbett asked belligerently.

'Oh, my God!' Rule turned round to face me but I was too busy trying to breathe through the choking yellow dust the truck in front was kicking up.

'What are you going to do?' Rule asked me.

'Oh, relax, I suppose. Have a decent meal. Drink a little. I don't know. Anything to get away from this lot. What about you?'

'I'm going to see a Brigadier friend of mine.'

I thought he must be joking. How could this poor Welsh miner possibly have anything to do with such a high and mighty person?

'Really? Are you applying for a commission?'

'It's not one of our brigadiers. It's a Salvation Army Brigadier. I knew him in Pontypridd and we've kept in touch. He's in Cairo now and I promised to join him on my first leave and help him start Bible-reading classes for men on leave there.'

I thought of the battle-weary soldiers who came down from the desert to let go and have a good time and I gave a short laugh.

'I wish you luck!' I must have sounded more than a little bitter because he didn't talk to me for a long time after that.

We stopped at Mersa Matruh for a rest and a meal.

'The Germans are really going it in Russia!' Corbett said. 'Latest news is they're meeting little opposition.'

It was shortly after the German invasion of Russia and we'd all gathered round the wireless truck to hear the big news. I think for most of us our hearts sank. The Germans struck at Russia with four mighty armies. They obviously wanted to be in Moscow before winter. In the south they were heading for the Caucasus and it looked as if Rommel wanted to go through Egypt and Palestine and link up with them in a huge pincer movement. Bearing in mind that the Germans had conquered most of Europe and the Americans hadn't yet entered the war, the general outlook for us at that time looked pretty grim. None of us, frankly, could see ourselves returning home to England for a long time to come, if ever. The Desert Army would probably fall back into Southern Africa.

'They have no idea how vast Russia really is,' I said.

'Even if they took Moscow, there are still thousands of miles to go beyond the Urals. The Russians have a huge Siberian Army which they have been building up and training for years – mainly for use against any threat from the Japanese. They'll throw that lot at the Germans if things get tough.'

'The invasion of Russia could be a blessing in disguise for us poor sods over here,' Corbett broke in. 'After all, imagine what would have happened to us if they'd sent those troops to North Africa.'

'The trick now is to knock them out of Africa before they beat Russia or they'll do just that,' I said

The conversation switched to civilian life and what we would do after the war. I told them I would probably have a look at South Africa.

'How about you, Rule?'

'I'll stick to mining,' Rule said. 'Those pit ponies are great pals of mine. Now and again I would bring them up to give them a break of course and I'd run them free in a big field. Don't know what they'd do without me!'

'What about you, Johnny?'

'I'll give up the docks, that's for sure.' Corbett screwed up his eyes against the sun. 'The desert is littered with broken-down trucks, lorries, tanks – especially tanks. And there'll be plenty more before this little lot's over. What will I do after the war? I'll go in for the salvage business. Scrap metal. I'll come back here and make my fortune!'

In Mersa Matruh we picked up seven more men who were also going on leave. Later we drove along the coast road, avoiding the MPs and hardly daring to stop anywhere, fearful of being told by somebody that our leave was cancelled. We had ten precious days but we knew that if there was any emergency at the front we'd be ordered back. This was always a danger for men on leave from the desert and it happened all too often.

Our driver wanted to pay a visit to Alex and stop overnight there but I told him to keep going. We trusted nobody, least of all the army.

At 'Halfway House' on the Alex to Cairo road there was a checkpoint and a couple of Red Caps came up to us. They were immaculate in their neatly-pressed uniforms, well-blancoed webbing, shiny buttons and polished boots. We looked, felt and must have smelt like tramps and I was uneasy. Even if our papers were in order they would be sure to make things difficult for us. Red Caps always did.

'I am the Sergeant in charge and we are a leave party on our way to the Royal Artillery camp at Almaza.'

The Red Caps told us to get out. Judging by the look on their faces they probably thought we were a bunch of deserters. In Mersa Matruh we called at the NAAFI and took on some crates of beer and all of us, except Rule, got through most of it. After all, it was a long and thirsty journey and then again we were on leave. When we climbed down the heat and the effects of the alcohol on our empty stomachs took its toll. Corbett, who had been putting it away more than anybody else, staggered across the road and proceeded to relieve himself, while the others, unable to stand about in the heat, sat down in the middle of the road.

I managed to stay on my feet by holding on to the side of the truck. I explained that we were a leave party down from the desert and I showed them my leave pass.

The Red Caps barely glanced at it. They informed us that we were improperly dressed as well as being drunk and disorderly, that we were all under arrest and they were going to telephone for a truck to come and pick us up. I tried to explain we had been in action for months and when our ten days were up we were going straight back into the line again, but I was wasting my time. We were just a bunch of drunken scarecrows but there was nothing that a little pack drill in one of their detention camps would not put right.

The road was busy and the MPs were continually having to attend to other vehicles. A big khaki-painted Humber drew up and a brigadier got out.

'What seems to be the trouble here?' He went across to one of the Red Caps. 'Who are these men and where are they from? Why can't you clear the road?'

'It's a leave party, sir. They're down from the desert. Field Artillery.' There was no mistaking his disgust.

'What's the hold up?'

'They're improperly dressed, sir, and they're drunk.'

I had already ordered everybody to get up and stand to attention. I saluted the Brigadier and explained who we were. I discovered that, like most Australian officers, he was much easier to talk to than our own lot and I got on very well with him. After questioning the two MPs, the Brigadier learned that the closest they had ever been to the front was, in fact, this roadblock.

'They've been up in the flaming bluey while you've been blancoing your bloody webbing, shining your blasted boots and swanning about in Cairo. Now let these men go and clear the bloody road!'

I had already pictured spending my leave behind barbed wire and now I began to breathe again. The MPs were all powerful and certainly nothing less than a full-blown Brigadier would have had much influence with them.

The Brigadier stood there while we climbed back into the truck. Our driver, who had probably drunk as much as any of us, seemed to have difficulty getting into gear, but we sped away at last, cheering wildly and yelling, 'Up the Australians!'

Almaza, the Royal Artillery base camp, was situated on the edge of the desert just outside Cairo. Here, incoming drafts from the UK and elsewhere were sorted out and posted to various units. The camp was divided into three branches of the Royal Artillery: Coast Defence, Anti-Aircraft and Field. For some reason discipline in the field artillery section did not seem to be as strict as in the rest of the camp where the drilling and shouting seemed to go on all day.

---

* Australians called the Desert the 'bluey' while British soldiers called it the 'blue'.

Maybe this was because many of the field gunners who passed through there belonged to the old regular British Army units that saw service in India and elsewhere. The NCOs were easier. They were tough sunburnt old soldiers and their whole manner was more casual, whereas the anti-aircraft drafts who were just out from England still clung to that regimental discipline which can make life so difficult. Whatever it was, life in the field artillery section at Almaza was certainly more pleasant.

After we had cleaned ourselves up and drawn our pay I suggested to Rule and Corbett that we find accommodation in the city itself. I explained that in a base camp like Almaza there was always the risk that our leave might suddenly be cancelled. If there was an emergency we might find ourselves being drafted to some other unit whereas if we were in the city we could enjoy every minute of our leave and return to our unit in good time. This suited Rule who said he would stay at the Salvation Army hostel in the town. Corbett, too, was enthusiastic but the problem was how to keep an eye on him and I felt myself responsible for getting him back safely with us at the end of our leave.

Corbett and I found rooms at the New Zealand Club in Cairo. The city was hot, smelly and noisy and the hooting of traffic was a twenty-four hour a day racket. At night I lay awake and listened to a cacophony of dance music from half a dozen different bands in my area alone. There was shouting, singing and fighting and to crown everything that infernal Arabic music which continued hour after exhausting hour throughout the night.

I decided to put off seeing Mary-Anne for a couple of days. After living rough with poor food and water and bouts of Gypo tummy and near dysentery I felt as if I had just climbed off the Inquisitorial rack. I needed rest and above all I wanted to be alone. The New Zealand Club was marvellous. I had my own room. There was a fan. The walls were painted a relaxing green and I could draw the shutters and lie in bed all day long if I wanted to.

Inevitably my thoughts came back to Mary-Anne and I wondered whether she had forgotten me. After all, Cairo was packed with troops from all nations and she could have been going out with somebody else all that time I was sweating it out in the blue. I finished my beer, poured myself a large whisky and tried to forget about her. Eight more days and I'd be back in the desert and God only knew if I'd ever come back to Cairo again.

I kept in touch with Corbett and Rule. Corbett usually drank too much and got into scrapes and it was all I could do to get him safely back to the New Zealand Club before the MPs arrived. Rule introduced me to his Salvation Army friends and tried to get me to join without success.

I did the usual sightseeing, including a visit to the Pyramids. At the Great Pyramid Arab guides offered to take people through the passages which led to the King's Chamber and I tagged on to one of these parties. A white-robed guide led the way inside with a flaming torch and sometimes he let out a bloodcurdling yell which echoed through the dark passages and mingled with the cries from the other guides. No doubt they hoped to receive an extra tip for scaring us when the tour ended.

Sometimes two of the parties would meet and there would be much joking and laughter before they squeezed past each other and continued on the way. It was on one of these meetings deep inside the Great Pyramid that I came face to face with Mary-Anne. She was on a guided tour with the medical staff from one of the hospitals. In the light of the torch, held high by the guide, she looked more beautiful than ever.

'Hell of a place to meet!' I said.

She stared at me. I must have been partly in the shadows because she came forward to peer at me, and then she smiled, and I could tell she was pleased to see me. She wore the same perfume. In that confined space it was glorious.

'Where on earth have you been?'

'Oh, up there,' I jerked a thumb over my shoulder. 'You know, mucking about.'

We stood and chatted there while both of the guided parties continued on their way. The light grew dim and suddenly we were alone and it was black as pitch. I don't think she was scared and, as for me, I just loved to be that close. At that moment I don't think I'd have minded if we had been shut up in there for ever. Reluctantly, I brought out my cigarette lighter.

'I'll lead the way. Keep your head down. We'll soon catch up with them.'

As we went on that same eerie yelling of the guides echoed along the passageways and after a while I took her by the hand. I had a good enough excuse. After all, we could have easily been separated. The lighter was only a cheap one from the NAAFI and I had used it mainly to light my pipe. Now the flame spluttered lower. There was not much petrol left. I tried to get her to talk a little to take her mind off things.

'We were living in Hobart, Tasmania. My mother was a nurse in the last war so I thought I'd have a go in this one.'

'And your father?'

'He was headmaster of a school there. His great interest was geology. He used to like going off to the mainland to look for gold and precious stones during the school holidays.'

'They must be longing for you to come back when this lot's over.'

'They're both dead, I'm afraid. It happened about three years ago. My mother was the first to go. My father didn't live long after that...'

I cursed myself for asking questions. I was supposed to be cheering her up. To make matters worse the flame spluttered finally and then went out, leaving us in pitch darkness. But she went on talking, perhaps to hide her sudden nervousness.

'After the war I plan to visit London. I've never been to England and I believe it's beautiful. I have an aunt in London and I shall stay with her for a few weeks and see the sights. Afterwards I'll go back to Australia. I'll live in Sydney, Canberra or maybe even Perth which I believe is lovely.'

It was possible to move but very slowly in the corridor. Anything was better than standing still so we began to edge our way in what we thought must be the right direction.

By this time I was beginning to have some fears myself particularly as we were one of the last parties to explore the inside of the Pyramid that day. I could think of nothing worse than being lost in that black maze of tunnels, counting the hours until, hopefully, another tour came along and rescued us the following day. I tried to console myself with the thought that there were worse places to spend the night with a girl like Mary-Anne. However, as luck, or ill luck, would have it, I glimpsed an oncoming light. Our guide, having counted the original party, realized we were missing, and was coming back to look for us.

So I will never know what it was like to spend a night in Cheops's chamber. In any case I think Mary-Anne was beginning to feel quite scared so maybe everything worked out for the best, although I did feel obliged to give the guide an extra tip.

We went for a walk in the sunshine and looked at the Sphinx.

I knew I must make a decision. I knew that if I wanted to see Mary-Anne again – if I didn't want her to walk out of my life for ever – it was up to me to do something about it. Besides, who knows, meeting her in the middle of the Great Pyramid like that might have been a good omen.

'Let's meet up for supper.'

I expected her to say she was otherwise engaged but to my surprise she liked the idea.

'Where do you suggest we meet?'

I was pleased to the point of feeling reckless. How could I offer anything to this lovely Australian girl but the very best?

'Shepheards?'

She thought I was joking but I'd said it and I would go through with it. I'd take her to Shepheards if it took all my pay.

'Six o'clock?' I decided to make it early. We could have a few drinks before the meal and then have a nice long evening.

Back at the New Zealand Club I tried to smarten myself up. My spare uniform was carted about in the desert with me and although it was cleaned and pressed, it probably still wasn't good enough for a place like Shepheards.

Shepheards Hotel was impressive. With its spacious rooms, English-style furniture and acres of plush carpeting, it was like a palace. Above all, there was peace. Here, as if its walls had been especially padded, one left the hot dusty streets and the incredible din outside. I felt a little nervous in those exclusive portals. Here I was surrounded by officers of impressive rank while all I had to support myself were my three stripes. I suddenly realized that Shepheards Hotel was for officers only! I had arranged to meet Mary-Anne here so there was nothing I could do about it. I would put on a bold front and try and pass myself off as a bearer of an important message for some top-ranking brass.

I went into the lounge, sank into an armchair and ordered a large John Collins. By the time Mary-Anne arrived I was halfway through another and everybody stopped looking at me and looked at Mary-Anne. If I didn't fit into Shepheards she certainly did. She was dressed in her army nursing uniform. She was very slim, her auburn hair shone, and those hazel eyes of hers made my heart lurch a little. We sat and chatted together and I began to relax. Left on my own I would probably have been thrown out of that place but Mary-Anne's presence there did something to lessen the tension.

The head waiter, however, like all head waiters, was not the sort of man to be fooled. He knew that I had gate-crashed Shepheards and he held his peace only because I happened to be British. At that time the British were fairly popular in Cairo, because we were spilling our blood to keep the invader out of Egypt, thus enabling the Egyptians, who never lifted a finger to help us, to carry on with their lucrative businesses, as well as enabling them to sleep safely at nights.

Also a little 'baksheesh' works wonders, especially with head waiters, and I decided that the only way to stop him staring at me with those dagger-like eyes of his was to give him a tip. I called him over, ordered another round and gave him the money and from that moment on I had no more trouble with the head waiter. The only thing that bothered me then was the bill I was running up and we hadn't even started on the food. Oh well, eat drink and all that....

The dining room was crowded. Three officers sat at the next table and one of them, a red-tabbed brigadier, scowled at me. I could tell he wanted me thrown out but maybe it was Mary-Anne who made him hesitate. He looked as if he wanted to get rid of me so that he could have her all to himself. I tried to reassure myself that the Brigadier was harmless. He could order me out but that would be embarrassing for his fellow diners – especially as I was in the company of that most prestigious of Cairo society, a very pretty army nursing sister.

I tried to think of Rod Wainwright and the Australian girl he once met in Cairo. Maybe Mary-Anne knew her.

'Do you happen to know Kate McDonald? She's an army nursing sister over here and she's Australian like yourself.'

'Kate McDonald? Yes, of course. Kate and I work at the same hospital. Why, is she a friend of yours?'

I laughed and shook my head. I told her how Rod had met her in Cairo and how much he was looking forward to seeing her again.

'Rod and I are on the same gun together and he's coming down here on leave when I get back. He's just crazy about Kate.'

'Oh dear!' Mary-Anne frowned. 'Sometime ago Kate met an officer from the Ninth Australian Division. His name is Dave Hilton and they've been seeing quite a lot of each other lately. In fact, I believe they're getting engaged.'

This would be a blow for Wainwright and she could see I was worried. 'It might be a good idea if you told him,' she said.

I forgot about the Brigadier, forgot that I was in Shepheards. If Rod thought Kate was no longer interested in him he'd probably cancel his leave. Rod and I had been through it together and now this woman was about to undermine his hard-earned leave. I cursed Rod's bad luck. I had the welfare of my men to consider and I was determined to put my oar in and do something about it.

'No. I'm not going to tell him. Rod fell for Kate in a big way and he talks of nothing else. If I told him about this man he'd cancel his leave and as likely as not he'd go to the dogs!'

I had an idea. It was a long shot but anything was worth trying. It was up to me to ensure that Rod not only took that leave but spent it happily. Heaven alone knew he needed it.

'Listen, could you arrange for her to meet me at the hospital tomorrow? Could the three of us have a talk together? I want you to try and get her to see Rod when he comes here on leave. I'll ask her to carry on as if nothing had happened – just for a few days. After all, he'll be back in the desert in no time at all.'

'I don't think Dave would like the idea and I suppose he'll have to come first!'

'No. I don't think he should, not in this case. I don't suppose Rod will get another chance to visit Cairo. Sooner or later there'll be a big push and we'll all end up on the other side of Africa. Come to think of it, goodness knows when you or I will meet up again either!'

As soon as I said it I could have kicked myself. She caught her breath and, somehow, that moment of sadness made her look more lovely than ever. Oh well, she must have been expecting me to go sooner or later: a soldier's life was not exactly a bed of roses.

'How about it then? Will you fix it up so I can see Kate tomorrow?'

'She has a coffee break mid-morning. Come on up to the hospital then and I'll see what I can do.'

It was time to go but I couldn't possibly pay the monstrous bill deposited in front of me. It was the red-faced brigadier who gave me an idea. He'd been drinking bucketfuls and when he got up to go to the toilet I called the head waiter over and pointed to his table. 'I'm a member of his staff,' I informed him briskly and I handed him back the bill. 'The Brigadier always settles for this sort of thing.'

He stood there google-eyed and undecided. Then he looked across at the brigadier's table where the people there were drinking their brandy and coffee and he must have realized that an NCO, a common sergeant, would hardly sit down to eat with such high and mighty people. I settled the matter, then, by rising and escorting Mary-Anne out of the hotel. Luckily, she saw the funny side of it and I believe that was because she was a big hearted Australian girl.

Kate McDonald could turn a few heads, mine included. She was tall and slim with long dark hair which bounced about on her shoulders when she walked. Close up she was a sensation but I thought those blue eyes of hers could be a little cold even when she smiled. I would say that beneath that charming exterior there was something else.

After Mary-Anne had introduced us, we talked about this and that and then I went straight to the point and asked her whether she could possibly see Rod when he came on leave to Cairo. Would she pretend, just for a few days, that nothing had happened between them?

'If he thought you were no longer interested in him he'd probably go to pieces. After all, he'll be back at the front in no time at all and sooner or later we're all likely to end up thousands of miles away from here'.'

'Lots of people change their minds,' she said. 'I was very fond of Rod but it was all rather a whirlwind affair and then he had to rush off back to his unit. Dave Hilton and I met at the Australian Club here in Cairo and we've been seeing each other almost every day...'

I had to be sympathetic. It was my only chance. 'Of course, I understand perfectly.' I tried to smile. 'All's fair in love and war... Look, you're a nurse. Couldn't you treat this as just another nursing job? Send the man away happy? Do a public relations job or something like that?'

I did my best to persuade her.

'What about Dave?' Kate protested. 'He doesn't stand for any nonsense. I'd find myself back on the shelf again if he saw me out with somebody else.'

'Tell him about Rod. Tell him he's only here on a few days' wretched leave and then he's back into the bluey again. If he's any man at all he'll go along with the idea. Do you mean to tell me Dave hasn't taken out other girls before? Listen, if you're straight with him, he'll admire you all the more.'

Kate looked at Mary-Anne who nodded her encouragement. 'Alright,' she said, 'I'll do it. I'll meet Rod and go out with him while he's on leave and I will try and explain it all to Dave.'

I breathed a sigh of relief. Maybe I was wrong about her after all. But, then again, who was I to judge Kate McDonald?

A strange silence hung over the desert and except for the occasional explosion as our guns worked out their schedule of harassing fire the whole front seemed to have settled down to a kind of stalemate – as if both sides had agreed, mutually, to take things easy in the appalling heat. Indeed, after Cairo with its interminable racket, the desert seemed positively peaceful. We spent much of our time on maintenance work and dug slit trenches and unloaded ammunition. Judging by the stuff coming up the coast road, there was soon going to be a big attack, and the great banks of dust in the west told us the Germans were preparing to have another go at us. The hot, thirsty, fly-ridden days fled and Rod returned from his leave in Cairo. I looked for signs of disappointment or stress in his face but he seemed quite happy.

'How did you get on? Did you see her?'

'Kate? She was wonderful,' he grinned widely, 'we spent almost every day together.'

'She still likes you?'

'Likes me?' he laughed. 'Tell you what, though, she did give me a bit of a turn once. She told me she'd been going around with an Aussie officer, a man called Dave Hilton. However, when she saw yours truly again, all sunburnt and handsome, she changed her mind!'

'Changed her mind?'

'Kate was perfectly frank about everything and she told me she and that Aussie were quite close together but, yes, she's changed her mind and fallen for me instead. I bought her a ring in Cairo and as soon as this lot's over we're going to be married.'

'Well, I'll be damned!' I thought I had heard everything.

All through that summer the build – up of armour continued while the churned-up dust hung like a fog in the sky. One evening we were detailed for patrol work. Normally this was a job for the infantry. However, since we were often out in front of the infantry – the more easily to deal with tanks – the job sometimes fell on us. This time eight men were detailed to go. Two men from each gun. I discovered I was on the list with Johnny Corbett. The general idea was to find out what the Germans were doing in front of us and we particularly wanted to discover the positions of some 88s causing so much havoc in our lines recently.

We couldn't patrol at night because of the danger of stumbling on to mines or booby traps. Besides, we needed maximum visibility to spot those 88s. A Lieutenant Baxter from one of our neighbouring batteries was in charge and we also had an engineer with us who was an expert on dealing with mines.

We started out at dawn so that the Germans would have the sun in their eyes. The desert here was flat but there were big rocks, thorn bushes and scrub plants as far as the eye could see and so we did have some cover. There were enemy patrols about, too, but I think our worst enemy was the heat and flies. Even at seven in the morning you could feel that first heat of the sun and you could tell that it was going to be another hell of a day. Also, trying to keep the flies off your face called for constant movement which, of course, increased the risk of being spotted by the vigilant German snipers. We carried Tommy guns and hand grenades and because water can be very heavy we had to cut down on that. I would have left behind one or two hand grenades and taken some extra water but Baxter, a keen type just out from England, shook his head.

'If you want a drink then take it off the Germans!'

The Lieutenant little knew that in the desert water can be more powerful than a weapon. If you were so thirsty you tried to take it off a German, he'd probably kill you first. He'd have the edge on you simply because he had the water. After we'd walked a short distance, we stopped and looked back. The sun was in our eyes of course but our guns had been so well camouflaged all we could see was the scrub and thorn and yellow desert.

'The Germans are good at that too,' the Lieutenant warned. 'Watch out or we'll be tripping over their own camouflage netting!'

From both sides now came that early morning roar of thousands of engines being warmed up, and the clouds of exhaust smoke spread across the desert like a fog. Soon, the sun, climbing steadily, would disappear into it and we'd be sitting ducks for the German snipers.

We skirted a minefield our engineer friend pointed out. Minefields were easier to spot from the air, he told us, especially in the desert, and from up there they sometimes resembled prehistoric workings or encampments. The German T-mines were a devil. They were buried at intervals in the sand. Then thin wire was strung out and attached to the detonator of each mine. The whole minefield might form a chessboard pattern stretching for hundreds of yards. The Germans, who were good toy makers, made it almost impossible for our engineers to defuse these contraptions. If they tried to unscrew the detonator or exert the slightest pull on those 'hair trigger' wires, the mine would go up with a roar. We carefully noted the position of this minefield so we could destroy it later with gunfire. The Germans were good at booby traps, too. Often we'd find a bar of chocolate, soap or a tin of beer or maybe a packet of cigarettes. Pick it up and you'd find a thin trail of wire but that was all you'd ever find, ever again…

Farther on we came across an old Italian-German graveyard. These men were buried hurridly, the few stones long since pulled aside by ghoulish scavengers. Of the dead, only their uniforms, chewed about and bleached almost beyond recognition, remained. The area here was pitted with shellholes and there was an old trench partly filled in with sand and barbed-wire entanglements running out in front. Tins, bottles, old newspapers and magazines, litter of every description was scattered about like a refuse dump.

Farther on we heard voices. A small party of Germans occupied part of that trench and were sitting about chatting and drinking their coffee as if the war were hundreds of miles away.

No doubt they thought it was a good idea to get away to their secret 'den' for a while. Anyway, they were lucky. Normally, we would have lobbed a couple of grenades in there and left them to it, but the last thing we wanted now was to have them all round our necks.

We crept away, from one thorn bush to another, until one of the 88s we were trying to find suddenly fired and scared the life out of us. The gun uias so cleverly camouflaged we stumbled up almost into their gun position. Sometimes it is difficult to distinguish a uniform in the bright glare of the desert, particularly as the Germans often wore the same kind of rough old shirt and shorts in the blistering summer as ourselves. And, of course, while on patrol we wore no give-away headgear. Anyway, if they saw us they didn't bother to challenge us. Maybe they thought we were that forward trench party returning for duty. We noted the position of the gun and Baxter, not content with finding just the one gun, led us on farther.

I could have told him it was a mistake. It was already past noon and we were right in among the bunkers and outposts of the German front line. Besides, it was painful crawling about on the flint-hard desert floor and the flies nearly drove us mad. Baxter told us to rub some dirt and sand into our clothes to dirty ourselves up and I think that saved us when, a few minutes later, we found ourselves in full view of a party of Germans who were busy working on a stretch of desert road about 300 yards away. However, they took no notice of us and must have thought we were just one of their returning patrols. We managed to distance ourselves gradually from the Germans until we could scramble away into the scrubland and return to our own lines.

The summer seemed to drag and the news bulletins got progressively worse. First of all, the Germans had pushed us out of Greece and then they launched a huge airbourne assault on Crete, which was evacuated at the end of May. Three weeks later the German armies invaded the Soviet Union and it seemed as if nothing could stop them advancing on Moscow in the north as well as pushing towards the Ukraine and the oilfields of the Caucasus.

We had been listening to the news at the wireless truck and afterwards Rod Wainwright and I walked back together to our own gun position.

'Don't you believe it!' Rod remarked. 'We in the west don't really know the Russians. They're part eastern and just as cunning. They are well aware the Germans are also moving hundreds of miles away from their railheads and main supply points and the more they can lure them on into those vast swamps and trackless forests the happier they'll be. Look at Stalin, that cunning old fox. He knows perfectly well that even if the Germans took Moscow they would not have conquered Russia by so much as one quarter! Besides, even if the Germans did win they could never hold down such a huge country for long, particularly as the inhabitants would conduct a merciless guerilla warfare!'

I knew that Rod had travelled a lot and I asked him if he had ever been to Russia.

'No, but I was up in Iraq once before I joined this mob, and I met some Russians there. One of them had once been a waiter in Soho and he spoke quite good English. I remember him telling me what a nation of mixed races they were. The north, for instance, and that includes Moscow, is practically a foreign country compared with, say, the Crimea or the Ukraine. The people in the north, he said, were rather cold and austere whereas in the south they were more warm-hearted and out-going and he told me a funny story to illustrate the point:

It was about a plane trip. The pilot was a Russian from the north. He had two passengers with him. One of the passengers was from the Crimea and the other from the Ukraine. They were flying over the Crimea and the man from that country threw great bunches of white carnations out of the window.

'The women in my country love white carnations!' he exclaimed.

The plane flew on over the Ukraine and the gentleman from that country flung out armfuls of yellow roses.

'Our women simply adore yellow roses!' he said.

The plane continued on into Russia and the two men asked the Russian: 'What's wrong with you? Don't Russian women love anything?'

'They love men from the Crimea and also men from the Ukraine,' says the Russian, 'so I don't know which of you to throw out first!'

CHAPTER THREE

Talk about a long hot summer. I think this one must have been all of them rolled into one. Here in the desert things were still quiet and we were sick and bored of maintenance work, parades and inspections. Our gun had been cleaned and oiled and the barrel pulled through so many times that I honestly believed we could have passed inspection for a Royal Salute in Hyde Park.

One evening I found myself chatting with some men from the Long Range Desert Group. This elite Commando force was raised for the purpose of operating deep into the desert and far behind enemy lines. Their job was to destroy ammunition dumps, petrol supplies, airfields and generally harass the enemy wherever they could be found. They were a tough adventurous bunch of men, volunteers all, who were trained to travel long distances with little food or water. This lot were here to get information on the twenty-five pounder field gun because they planned to take one of these guns with them for a special job on their next trip. The Battery Commander asked me to show them round and give them some instruction on the weapon.

Their leader was a Lieutenant, a tall rangy Australian named Tom Longford. Everybody called him Long Tom. I noticed that one side of his face was pock-marked as if he had once had smallpox, but I learned later that a grenade burst close to him in some earlier action. The Lieutenant had a habit of putting his hand up to that cheek when he had a problem. There were ten others, a mixed assortment of British, Australian and New Zealand soldiers.

One day I sat them down in front of a blackboard and easel and gave them a lecture on the science of ballistics. I could soon tell that most of them, especially the rough necks from the outback, were finding the subject difficult to grasp and at last Long Tom interrupted me.

'Just show us how to fire the thing. We'll be using open sights where we're going anyway!'

So we all trooped out to where the twenty-five pounder was sitting, looking rather silent and sinister. They were not used to being right on top of a field gun when it went off and, tough men though they were, they jumped a bit when it gave that nasty ear-splitting slam. We had plenty of targets to practise on out there and for the next few days I did my best to instruct this motley crew on the rudiments of gunnery. It was during this training that a wild idea began to form in my mind.

It happened that the CO had recently suggested that the gun crews should get more experience at 'sniping'. This was the term used when a gun team went off on its own, independent of the battery, to shoot up targets at close range. They would then move on quickly to the next position before the enemy could get on to them. The war in the desert seemed to have settled down to stalemate and, as I said before, I was a little bored with the endless routine and would have given anything to get away for a change. If there was any adventure left in this miserable war, I told myself, it would surely be found with the Long Range Desert Group. I would tell the Colonel that I would get plenty of experience at 'sniping' if I could go with the LRDG for a while.

'Right,' I said to Long Tom, 'I've shown you a few tricks. All you need now is an old hand at the game like me to come along with you.'

At first he thought I was joking. 'Are you tired of life or something?' He told me some of the things the LRDG had got up to, and did his best to put me off, but I was determined to go, if he would have me, and I pointed out to him that my experience as a gunner would be invaluable. When he was sure that I was serious he grinned enthusiastically. 'Could you swing it?'

'I think so. That is, if you could have a word with my CO too. Tell him you would like an experienced field gunner to go with you on your next trip.'

In the end, much to my surprise, it worked and the Colonel said that, as things were fairly quiet, I could go. And because the idea seemed to fit in with his recent plans for the gun crews to have more experience at 'sniping', I was to report to him on my return and describe how the Battery could profit by such an exercise. Furthermore, I could take one of my own men with me, providing he was a volunteer. I made a quick decision and had a word with Corbett. Rod Wainwright, my Number Two, would be left in charge. It was mid-July. 'Be back before October,' the Colonel said. I could guess why. Everybody knew that things would start moving again in the autumn.

Corbett had already made some friends among the LRDG men and he was only too pleased to get away. He was the sort of man who would go through hell and high water for some real excitement and this was why I chose him. Corbett and I left with the LRDG bunch the following day. I think my crew were sorry to see me go. Rod was well liked but nobody knew how he would turn out as Number One. Better the devil you know and all that.

Long Tom told me that he would have to go back to Mersa Matruh for further instructions and briefing, also to pick up the rest of the party including our supplies and equipment and the twenty-five pounder field gun. He explained that the LRDG worked under the strictest security and even he did not know where they were bound for after that.

The Germans operated a similar Commando force called the Brandenburgers and these men made many daring raids far behind the British lines. They blew up ammunition dumps, shot up airfields and troop columns and sometimes penetrated almost as far as Cairo. The German espionage system in North Africa was uncanny. Everybody knew that Cairo was riddled with spies and people who would do anything for money, and they sometimes knew about an impending British attack even before the commander in the field. Long Tom told me that on more than one occasion the Brandenburgers had got wind of their plans and the LRDG column had had to fight its way out of some ambush.

We took the coastal road to Mersa Matruh while the long columns of tanks, guns and lorries roared by endlessly on the other side. Leaving your friends and everything you have lived with for such a long time can be a depressing business, and I began to wonder whether I had not made a hasty decision because I had been bored. Here I was with some crackpot outfit and a decidedly uncertain future and, as I stared at the endless expanse of yellow sand, the prospect of seeing my own unit again, let alone Mary-Anne, did seem a little remote.

We drove through Mersa Matruh and along a barren stretch of coastline until we came to a collection of dilapidated looking ex-Italian army huts which seemed to be completely deserted. However, the first hut we entered turned out to be a fully furnished office complete with British and Australian office staff. There were huge maps of North Africa on the walls and the busy chatter of typewriters mingled with the constant ringing of telephones. The men milling about were a bearded scruffy-looking lot dressed in shabby, almost unrecognizable, uniforms. Close by were the sleeping quarters, canteen, cookhouse and a hut which contained a veritable arsenal of weapons. This collection of apparently deserted looking huts was the LRDG's general headquarters. Long Tom, who had a slight limp and carried a walking stick, came up to me.

'Anybody can tell you're a regimental man. Forget to shave. Dirty yourself up a little. When we go into town we want people to think we're a no-good bunch of behind the line shirkers. So try and look the same as us or we'll all end up in the bloody creek.'

We stayed in Mersa for ten days. At first Corbett and I were inclined to stick together. The LRDG were a pretty rough lot and although Corbett, a Geordie, could mix it with the worst of them, he wanted to avoid a fight for fear of being thrown out of the expedition.

Long Tom introduced us to the men who would work with us on the twenty-five pounder. There was Frank Buckley, a sheep farmer from Australia. Lank and weatherbeaten, he had about him a perpetual air of cynicism as if everything was 'old hat' and he'd seen it all before. Maybe those sheep-shearing days of his gave him an idea because he cut off most of his hair for comfort and hygiene in the desert.

Sid Plummer was a Cockney. Small, wiry and humorous. He was one of those know-all types who could tell you what to do about almost anything. He was a good mechanic though and could strip down an engine and put it together in record time.

Lance Corporal Butt. Ex-schoolmaster. He was a great man on Shakespeare and could recite whole chunks of it. He joined a City of London territorial regiment and then volunteered for the LRDG soon after he got out there. He could have had a commission but was planning to write a book and wanted to see the rough side of the army first. Some say his stripe was just a 'protection' stripe, but

I don't think so because here he was, a volunteer with the LRDG. Butt. I had seen his type before. Strange how they seem to turn up in outfits like this one.

Then there was Corporal Bill Jackson. A silent pipe-smoking old regular whose hair was bleached almost the colour of sand by the sun. He had served in India and Palestine and was inclined to hold himself aloof from the rest of us. 'Daddy Bill' we called him because he was older than any of us.

Jock McAlister was an ex-seaman and a criminal type in and out of jail in Civvy Street. Safe breaking was his speciality, that and the de-fusing of mines and booby traps which, of course, go fairly well together and called for the same kind of knack. He had another useful qualification. He was utterly fearless. The LRDG were quick to sign him up.

Then there were twenty other men including Long Tom. All of them rough mercenary types, the kind of men I suppose you'd find in an outfit like the French Foreign Legion. Now that I had settled in I was glad I'd come. A pity to live out your life and never be in on a thing like this.

One day Johnny Corbett came up to me with a big grin on his face. 'Just heard how good the pay is with this lot.'

I was pleased too. All the same, there was something slightly ominous about his remark and my spirits sank a little when I began to wonder whether any of us would get a chance to spend it.

I studied map reading, attended lectures on how to survive in the desert for long periods without food or water, and underwent a short intensive course on the laying of mines and booby traps. In turn I was able to give some instruction on the twenty-five pounder field gun. We ran the gun out into the desert and fired off a lot of shells to the huge delight of the LRDG men. We rigged up a dummy target by tying some oil drums together and towing them across the desert at the end of a long line while we shot at them over open sights. The LRDG men became so enthusiastic with each man wanting to take his turn at driving the truck or firing the gun that we spent most of the day out there.

In the last afternoon some armoured vehicles came racing out from Mersa Matruh to find out what the noise was all about. Apparently somebody thought Rommel's tanks had broken through and the town was about to be besieged.

For the next couple of weeks we ate well and enjoyed ourselves. Sometimes we went to the NAAFI cinema in Mersa Matruh but more often than not we drove down to the white sandy beach and bathed in the blue Mediterranean.

On the day of our departure we learned our operation was code named BOOMERANG. Two armoured cars, two fifteen-cwt trucks and a couple of two – tonners, one of which was towing the twenty-five pounder field gun, drew up outside the headquarters hut. Each of the vehicles was fitted with deep – tread tyres and was freshly camouflaged with a sandy-coloured paint. The trucks were loaded with supplies of food, weapons and ammunition. In the desert we used to tie our water cans in front of a vehicle for maximum coolness. These trucks had cans hanging all over them. And petrol – I have never seen so many tins. Somehow, I didn't think we were going down to the beach for a swim.

We had meetings in the Operations Room all that day and for the first time we learnt about our immediate destination. We were to travel due south for about fifty miles until we came to the Qattara Depression. We'd continue along the edge of the Depression for another seventy miles. The Group would then head westward for about eighty miles to Siwa Oasis, No further information was given to us. Security was such that even at this stage nobody told me that Siwa, which lay deep in the south, was the Long Range Desert Group main centre for most of its operations against the Germans. However, we all knew that our route was chosen deliberately to put the Germans off the scent. After all, who on earth would guess that the LRDG would travel via the Qattara Depression in order to operate behind the German lines?

We left Mersa Matruh under a full moon that night and drove southward. There are no roads in this part of the desert and the surface varies from soft almost, impenetrable, sand to hard stony ground. At dawn we reached the northern rim of the Qattara Depression. This vast geological basin in the middle of the Egyptian desert stretches for almost 200 miles from north to south and covers an area of some 26,000 square miles. It is nearly seventy miles wide and lies hundreds of feet below the level of the Mediterranean sea. The floor of the Depression consists of quicksand, salt, desert and mud flats. The Depression is feared, impassable and, the Arabs say, haunted. Nothing can live in this burnt-out and blasted Death Valley.

Yet even this place has its moments of sublimity, and sunrise, for instance, made us all want to stop and stare. The first rays strike down to the salt at the bottom where a million shafts of brilliant light transform the rocks and ravines into a veritable fairyland. There is movement among the shadows and the sentinel pillars seem to come to life. When the sun climbs higher the magic disappears and the valley begins to shimmer in the appalling heat of another day.

We rested and had a 'brew up'. There was no wood about so we made a fire in the usual way. We built a small circle of stones and poured a little petrol on to the sand in the middle. The fire burnt long enough for us to make tea. I found myself sitting next to Lance Corporal Butt. I tossed a stone over the edge of the escarpment.

'One of these days they could fill it up.'

'Fill it up?' Butt paused with his mug. 'What with?'

'Water. One day they could turn the tap on and let the Med into that basin. They'd filter out the salt and, Bob's your uncle, there's a big new lake and everything would be green around here. Furthermore, by exploiting the drop between the Med and the Depression they could have a big new source of hydro-electric power too.'

Butt laughed. 'They'd have to dig some sort of canal first.'

'They dug the Suez all those years ago. Think what they could do with modern machines today and it doesn't have to be nearly as wide as the Suez. Besides, the distance from the Med at its nearest point is only half the length of the Suez Canal.'

'It'd take a long time to fill up,' Butt muttered, 'but a new lake? Come to think of it, that's quite an idea. The Nile is always running low because of drought.' He grinned. 'The Gypos would be delighted if you came up with an idea like that.'

Long Tom told us that, although it was unlikely we should meet any enemy troops so far south, we should, nevertheless, keep a sharp lookout. You never knew what the Brandenburgers were up to, he said. They could easily be travelling via the Qattara Depression themselves en route for one of their raids behind our lines.

We drove along the edge of the Depression under a bright moon. It was like a journey across some long-dead planet. Sometimes the crags and pinnacles of rock which formed the edge of the escarpment gave way and we could see right down to the petrified sea of sand.

We headed south for two more days and then turned westward for Siwa. The desert here was flat and flint hard and mirages were common, not the lush – green – oasis – looking kind but shimmering lake-like apparitions which recede and then vanish as you drive towards them. Every few miles we had to stop to cool the engine. All we could see was a hard blue sky and an eternity of yellow sand. The heat was like a wall – even the bodywork of the truck was too hot to touch – and the constant glare made your head ache and your eyes sore. And the flies seemed to appear out of nowhere. It was impossible to keep them away and they could give you a painful nip. When we made camp we had to burn our empty tins, refuse and the latrine trenches with petrol.

One evening it was very warm, the moon like a lantern and the desert still. We listened to the news on the radio. It was strange that out here in the middle of North Africa we could hear the BBC announcer all the way from London. The Germans were unleashing an inferno of death and destruction from the sky – London, Coventry, Bristol… The German armies, already on the Smolensk–Moscow highway, were pushing even closer to Moscow. Hardly a mention was made of the desert campaign – that big battlefield where the British Army still fought alone. And as for the Long Range Desert Group – we sometimes felt that we were the Legion of the Lost.

Corporal Jackson, the old regular, knocked out his pipe and went to fetch his bedding roll. We kicked some loose stones away and shook out our blankets before going to bed. We were all scared of scorpions, especially the black kind, and then there were the tarantulas.

I had seen Siwa Oasis on the map but never dreamed I'd ever visit such a remote place. Butt, the ex-schoolmaster, said that if we had the time he would like to explore some Roman ruins which he heard were there and I said I would go along with him. We had been following one of the old caravan trails through some hilly country and were descending an escarpment when we saw the oasis beneath us; a vista of palm trees, mud – brick huts and green irrigated land. We by-passed the main settlement and wound our way through a narrow defile in the hillside until we came to an open area of ground which was almost totally surrounded by cliffs. Long Tom pointed to some Bedouin tents at the foot of the cliffs.

'Our administration offices,' he said, 'practically impossible to spot from the air. Even if they could see us, they would only think we were an Arab settlement.'

Immediately behind the tents were some caves that ran deep into the cliff face and in here the LRDG stored their arms and equipment. There was nothing to show that this was an army base, and even if the Brandenburgers were to stumble on to the place they'd probably turn round and drive out again.

We put our transport under camouflaged netting and tried to be as inconspicuous as possible with only two or three men being allowed into the village at a time. Arabs talk and there was no point in advertising our presence there especially as we were about to go on an important raid.

One day we learned that our first target was to be the German airfield at El Agheila on the Mediterranean coast of Libya. We were then to proceed to Agedabiya and blow up the enemy petrol dump there. The distance from Siwa to El Agheila via the El Ergh Oasis is about 350 miles. Agedabiya is another fifty miles along the coast.

'If we can get that twenty-five pounder close enough we'll save ourselves a lot of trouble,' Long Tom said. 'They're not likely to have many troops there and they'll hardly expect us to pay them a visit at Agedabiya the same day!'

'After that?' Frank Buckley asked. 'After that, we get out'.'

We were in Siwa for ten days during which Butt and I took every opportunity to explore the place. We discovered that the oasis had a population of about 3,500 Berber-speaking people and was about seven miles long and five miles wide. There were many springs and the area was green and fertile with olive trees and date palm plantations. We learned that Siwa was the ancient Egyptian seat of the oracle temple of Amon and Alexander the Great was welcomed there in 331 BC as a son of Amon. The ruins of the temple had fourth-century BC inscriptions and we found many Roman remains. We discovered that the first European to reach Siwa was William George Brown, a British traveller, in 1792.

Butt and I enjoyed going into the market place to buy eggs, bread and fresh figs and oranges and once, when Butt examined the change which an old leathery faced Arab stallholder had given him, he discovered a Roman coin. It had evidently been circulating as legal currency for almost 2000 years in that remote place.

It was tough leaving that green paradise and starting out on the 200-mile haul to El Ergh. On the third day, after we had joined one of those ancient caravan trails which come up from the deep south, we came across the remains of an Arab camp. The fires were still smouldering and there was a lot of camel dung where they put their animals for the night. We could tell that a big party of Arabs had camped there.

We caught up with them later that day. Their camels were piled high with their possessions and it looked as if an entire village was on the move. We made no attempt to avoid them. They must have heard us coming and had probably seen us anyway.

Long Tom, who knew a little Arabic, sought out their leader. He learned that the well which their village had depended upon had dried up and they had travelled hundreds of miles already in their search for a new home. We had been told to be wary of all Arabs because you never knew which side they were on, although it was generally safe to assume they'd be on the winning one.

Since they were travelling in the same direction as ourselves and we didn't want them to tell the Germans they had seen us, Long Tom ordered some tins of bully beef and tobacco to be distributed among them. These Arabs had never seen bully beef or western tobacco before and in return they gave us a supply of fresh fruit and told us where we could find some good wells of fresh water.

After we left them we ran into a sandstorm. It was like a tidal wave, a holocaust of sand swept up by scorching winds from the south and for twenty-four hours we were at a standstill while we groped about in a world of driving sand. Sand, which we breathed, got into our food and drink and stripped the paint off our vehicles. When the storm moved on we discovered that our twenty-five pounder gun had disappeared and at first we thought it must have been buried. However, the other vehicles were still there and Long Tom, after looking about him, made the startling announcement:

'It's been stolen. Those bloody Arabs have nicked our gun!'

There seemed to be no other explanation. Nothing would have been easier for the thieves to creep up in that sandstorm, unhook the gun, tie it to a camel and make off.

'What on earth would they want with a twenty-five pounder?' one of the men asked.

'They'd use it for their inter-tribal wars and raiding parties,' Long Tom said. 'They haven't got any ammunition but there's plenty lying about in the dumps up north!'

He cursed. He'd have a job living this one down. If he didn't get that gun back he'd be the laughing stock of the service. A twenty-five pounder field gun filched under their noses by a gang of Arabs.

We drove all the way back to the Arab column where their leader checked and discovered that four of his men were missing. These men, he explained, were strangers to his own tribe and they had asked him for permission to accompany his caravan across the Great Sand Sea which lay across his route.

'It looks as if they were just a bunch of robbers,' he apologized to Long Tom. 'If they have taken your gun, they will be punished.'

He lent us some men, all good trackers who were well versed in the ways of the desert, and we found them that same day. They had not only stolen our gun but two of the camels belonging to the caravan as well. The robbers abandoned the gun and fled but we caught their leader.

Long Tom, anxious to make up for lost time, ordered us to keep driving until we were back on schedule, so we drove all night. There was still a moon and we made good progress and at dawn we stopped for a brew up and a bite to eat. I was enjoying a mugful of tea when the sound of an engine made me look up. An armoured car stood there on a ridge of sand not a hundred yards away and the dirty black cross on its side made me spill my drink.

At first they couldn't tell whether we were friend or foe. There was not much paint left on our vehicles and we looked a pretty scruffy lot. Except for the twenty-five pounder which was sandwiched between two of our trucks there was little to show that we were British. The driver shouted something to us and when Long Tom yelled back a greeting in German he became suspicious and drove off. Long Tom then studied the desert through his glasses. The heat shimmer was deceptive but he told us that he could see at least four more armoured cars out there.

'It's the Brandenburgers. Just our luck running into them out here.'

The armoured cars, which had been milling about, now spaced themselves out and came towards us, the dust streaming out behind them like smoke from a flotilla of destroyers.

'Take post!' Long Tom yelled. 'Get that gun up here!'

We rushed to unhook the gun from the truck and by the time we manhandled it up the slope and got it into position those armoured cars were only 300 yards away. The ammunition truck bogged down halfway up the slope and we had to form a line and pass the shells to the gun by hand. Corbett and McAlister worked like demons to unload the shells from the ammunition truck.

Buckley threw open the breech and Plummer thrust in a shell while Jackson, still puffing away at his pipe, stood ready to ram it home. Butt, who was layer, stared across the open sights at the oncoming armour.

'On target!'

Then everything seemed to go wrong. Jackson, with the rammer, was trying to ram the shell into the breech.

'The bloody thing won't go in!' he yelled and he repeatedly struck the base of the shell.

I knew all about the danger of premature bursts. Dirty shells, torn driving bands, faulty fuses and as Number One I was constantly on the look out for these things. One of the greatest dangers was 'double shotting' a gun. This sometimes happened when a gun crew, often too tired to think properly, tried to ram home a round when there was still a shell in the breech. In those split seconds I thought we had the same problem.

'Stand fast!'

I pushed Jackson and Plummer out of the way and pulled out the shell. Then I put my arm into the breech and pulled out a fistful of sand. Sand! We had been in such a hurry to get our gun back from the Arabs and make up for lost time we forgot about that sandstorm. And because the gun is usually towed with its barrel more or less elevated the sand was still there. The barrel was choc-full of the stuff.

By now the armoured cars were really close so we opened up with our machine guns. Some of our men were distributing grenades and Long Tom gave the order to fix bayonets. We also managed to get one of our captured Italian Breda guns into action. When these things open up you know you've got a deterrent. However, the heavy bullets, which were more like small shells, ricocheted off those armoured cars and hummed and buzzed in all directions and nearly did for us too. Then the Germans, spotting our twenty-five pounder and not wanting to take any chances, turned round and made off across the desert. Although the Brandenburger column was much stronger than us, a twenty-five pounder field gun was something to reckon with. Little did they know that it was out of action.

'Live and let live'.' I said to Long Tom. 'Yes, that's what it probably adds up to. I expect they've got a job to do same as us and they don't want to foul up their chances any more than we do,' he wiped the sweat from his face. 'What the hell went wrong with that gun of yours anyway?'

'It was that sandstorm. The barrel was choc a bloc with sand.'

Long Tom shook his head. 'Talk about the sands running out. That stuff almost did for you lot!'

He kept us there until the barrel of our gun was so clean it hurt our eyes to look inside it.

We pushed on westwards. We knew the Germans would have reported our presence there as we had reported theirs, but the desert is a big place and we could only hope that they had no idea of our destination or the targets we were after. The endless days of brassy blue sky, scorching sun and an eternity of shimmering sand can get you down and every day we looked forward to the relief which came with nightfall; moreover, we were rationed to one gallon of water per man per day and this had to do for washing, shaving and making tea. Sometimes we were so thirsty we felt like gulping down the lot in one glorious go.

We usually made camp fairly early in the evening so that we had plenty of time to clean ourselves up, check our arms and equipment and have some sort of evening meal. Long Tom told us that, whenever possible, we should wash and shave every morning. If we had gone all night without sleep, he said, then the benefits of a wash and a shave counted for two hours' sleep. A good breakfast with a mug of strong sweet tea would equal another two hours. I had to admit that it helped but I think most of us would have preferred the real thing.

One evening I was sitting next to 'Daddy Bill' Jackson. He was drinking Chianti captured from the Italians and I offered him some tobacco. I asked him what made him join up.

'I wanted to find somebody.' The hatred in his voice was unmistakable and I fell silent. I didn't want to be personal but on the other hand he must have known that he couldn't leave it at that. He took another swig and began to unwind a little. He described how, just before the war, he fell in love with a girl called Sally. Everything was fine and they were going to be married. However, Jackson, then a travelling salesman who was often away from home for long periods at a time, discovered that another man, Paul Reynolds, a wealthy playboy type, had been forcing himself upon her. One day Reynolds, who had been drinking, took the girl out in his car and they had an accident. Sally was killed.

'I tried to find him,' Jackson said. 'I hunted for him all over the place and then I discovered that he joined the army to try and get away from me. In the end I joined up too. The army's not all that big. One of these days I'll run up against him.'

'But what are you doing in the LRDG? You're not likely to find anybody stuck out here!'

'That's what you think. Where would you want to hide if you knew somebody was after you? Besides, I knew the Commando training would come in handy. One of these days I'll bump into him. Maybe it'll be in Cairo or Alex or even on a jaunt like this one. The army is like a prison. You can't get out, especially if there is a war on, so that narrows down my field of search!'

My pipe had gone out and I re-lit it. I was beginning to believe that our 'Daddy Bill' was not such a benevolent 'Daddy' after all!

'What will you do if you find him?'

Jackson didn't reply. He just looked at me as if I'd asked a silly question.

CHAPTER FOUR

El Ergh was a perfect example of the traditional oasis. Green, with natural springs and surrounded by palm trees, it was a paradise. When we made camp there a great weight seemed to fall away from us and we emptied the stale tepid sandy liquid out of our canteens and filled them with cool clear spring water. Now we could wash, shave and drink as much water as we liked.

At El Ergh we spent a couple of days practising what we had to do at El Agheila and we went off into the desert with the twenty-five pounder and banged off a lot of rounds until the local Arabs became quite scared. Anyway it suited us to get rid of some ammunition and lighten our trucks a little because we would have to be pretty mobile when we got to the airfield.

Two days after we left El Ergh we were hit by the Khamseen, that wind which whips up the sand and drives it across the desert in choking yellow clouds. The Khamseen can blow for hours or days. Wind up the windows of your vehicle and the sand gets inside.

It gets under the bonnet and into the engine and gearbox. It seeps through every crack and cranny in the vehicle. It gets into your eyes, nose and mouth and you feel it on your teeth. There is sand in your food and when you reach for your precious water it is just a gritty lukewarm swill. If you are travelling in the back of the truck you pull your groundsheet over your head and muffle your face with some article of clothing but it is never any use. You are jolted about in a world of suffocating sand and all you can do is curse and pray for the storm to end.

We reached El Agheila three days later. The sound of engines warming up and planes taking off and landing helped to guide us towards the airfield. We found what cover we could and put camouflage netting over the vehicles and waited for darkness. Some planes flew overhead but they paid no attention to us. The gun was well camouflaged and they must have thought we were one of the service or supply units which operated close to a busy airfield.

'We will get as close as possible with the twenty-five pounder and shell any aircraft we see on the ground,' Long Tom said. 'We will then lift our fire on to the hangars, workshops and airfield buildings.'

We got little sleep that night. Our trucks were topped up with petrol and the engines checked ready for a quick getaway after the operation. Shells for the twenty-five pounder were transferred to one of the lighter trucks which would also be used for towing the gun into action. Rifles and Bren guns were checked and extra magazines loaded and made ready. Boxes of hand grenades were opened up and the contents distributed.

Late that evening Long Tom and I took a small party and crept up close to the airfield. There were several planes out there and we could tell by their silhouettes that they were Messerschmitts, Stukas and Dorniers. We could just make out the shadowy figures of the guards. When we got back Long Tom held a brief conference.

'We'll wait for sun up. It'll be right in their eyes. We'll get in close with the twenty-five pounder and blast those planes off the ground. Then the truck parties will go in with grenades to mop up. Remember, if there are any planes left that can still take off and fly we'll be for it!'

Long Tom had tied a small Union Jack to his walking stick. 'If you get into trouble – if there are any problems – make for this flag!'

We spaced our vehicles out at fifty-yard intervals and then the twenty-five pounder was hooked on to our truck and we drove out in front for a short distance. I wondered what the chances were. We had no idea how strongly fortified the place was. All we could do was get in there quickly and destroy as many planes as possible and then get out.

At first light we were ready to go. I sat next to McAlister who was to do the driving. The rest of my crew, Plummer, Corbett, Butt, Buckley and Jackson, were ready with their automatic weapons in the back of the truck. McAlister brought out his pipe, stuffed it with tobacco and lit it. He might have been waiting for the traffic lights to change. The sun rose blood red and almost immediately you could feel its warmth. Soon it would be like an oven. I could see Long Tom going about unconcernedly from one vehicle to the other discussing the situation and giving out last-minute orders. I thought he looked a little ridiculous with that Union Jack on the end of his walking stick.

The aerodrome was still quiet and nobody seemed to have noticed us. Then, when the sun had climbed a little higher, Long Tom pulled himself up into his armoured car and gave the signal for us to move forward.

McAlister put his foot down but it took some time for our truck with its load of men and ammunition and the heavy gun behind to get going. At last he got it into top gear and the gun started to jump about and make a racket over the loose stones and rocks as we accelerated towards the airfield. Behind us the other vehicles were racing, too, and great clouds of dust spread out and hid the sun. The Germans spotted us quickly and machine-gun bullets whined about us and ricocheted off our trucks. McAlister had got a good speed up and I told him to stop before we ended up in the officers' mess because if we didn't get that gun into action now we never would. He slammed on the brakes so hard that the gun slewed round and nearly overturned. We jumped down to uncouple it from our truck but discovered that the release mechanism had jammed. Then a Klaxon alarm started to blast out from the airfield buildings and troops came running on to the tarmac. I heard an aircraft engine cough and then roar. There were a dozen planes on the ground and if we didn't destroy them they would take off and destroy us. Suddenly the squeal of tank tracks and a German Mark IV loomed up on the airfield perimeter.

Long Tom was yelling at us. 'Get that gun into action'.'

'The gear's jammed. We can't unhook it!'

'Then fire the bloody thing as it is. Get a shell in there and blast those planes off the ground!'

It was a crazy idea to fire that gun while it was still hooked up to a truck, and I don't suppose it had ever been done in the history of artillery, but we could still elevate or depress the barrel so we just had to take a chance. We were all worried about the kick-back, and whether the gun would wrench itself free and somersault on top of us, because when it is fired normally the trail digs into the ground and softens the recoil.

Corbett and Butt started to hand down some shells from the top of the truck. Plummer yanked open the breech and Jackson rammed home a round. Buckley, twirling the wheel furiously, was peering over the open sights. 'The tank or the planes?'

'The planes damn it – that's what we came for!' The Germans were firing tracer at us. It was like watching an oncoming stream of meteorites and their fire was so accurate that I cannot understand why they didn't blast us off the desert.

'On target!'

'Stand clear!'

I gave a tug at the lanyard and jumped away myself. The gun fired and the trail smashed onto the rear of the truck, pushing the vehicle back several yards and sending Corbett and Butt off the top and sprawling among the ammunition.

'Load!'

The breech clanged like a ship's bell.

'Stand clear!'

'Fire!'

Black smoke from the airfield told us we had hit one of the planes. Next time we fired the force of the recoil tore the coupling completely off the truck and in spite of everything it was a great relief. Now at least we were back on home ground as it were and could manoeuvre and fire the thing as it was meant to be fired. From then on it was like a shooting gallery and soon half a dozen planes stood burning on the tarmac while the exploding ammunition sent bullets whizzing in all directions.

Meanwhile Long Tom's men were blazing away with machine guns and getting ready to move in closer. An 88 put an end to all that with a boom and an earsplitting crash. The gun, which had opened up from somewhere behind the airfield buildings, had scored a direct hit on our 2-ton lorry which was stacked with our reserve supply of twenty-five pounder ammunition. The petrol tank exploded and the vehicle became a mass of flames. I saw two men jump down from the cab and run for their lives. Long Tom saw the danger and signalled for everybody to get clear. We found some rope, tied the trail of the gun to the rear bumper of our truck and tried to put some distance between us and that potential landmine. But the 88 had got the range and another shell blew our gun over on to its side. This had the effect of throwing out an anchor and the truck was dragged back almost to a standstill, the gun came up against a rock and the tow rope snapped. I jumped down and ran round to the back of the truck; the men up there were badly jolted about and bruised. Plummer and Jackson, hit by shrapnel, were dead.

There was smoke everywhere and I couldn't see Long Tom's armoured car. The German Mark IV was weaving about, its gun blazing, and I noticed that two more of our vehicles were on fire; the remaining 2-tonner and a 15-hundredweight truck. The tank was coming straight for us and was level with the blazing 2-tonner when that load of twenty-five pounder shells went up with an explosion which tore the sky apart. We threw ourselves flat as shards of steel and chunks of shell casing flew over our heads. The tank took the full blast and was blown on to its side. Black smoke started to pour out of it and then there was another explosion and the turret flew off into the sand.

The 88 was still shelling us and we wanted to get out of there before the Germans thought of sending over air bursts, so we backed up the truck and went to take a look at the gun. The wheels had been blown off and there was a great hole in the shield where the open sights should have been. The 88 shells were dropping unpleasantly close and we were about to climb on board our truck and get out of there when Long Tom drove up in his armoured car and jumped down. His face was streaked with dirt and his clothes were smouldering. He looked as if he had just come out of a fire.

'Five of my men are dead. All we've got left is a couple of armoured cars and that truck of yours!'

He stood there thumping the smoke out of his clothes. 'Well, what are you waiting for? Hitch that gun up and get out of here!'

'Look at it. It's not fit for the scrapyard!'

Long Tom went across and gave the gun a kick. 'The barrel's alright isn't it? So is the breech mechanism and I notice you've still got some reserve ammo in the back of your truck.'

I thought he must be joking but who was I to argue? We lashed the trail of the gun to the bumper of our truck and drove off. The barrel dug into the ground and churned the sand and stones up like a plough but we managed to follow his armoured car – direction Agedabiya and that petrol dump we were supposed to blow up. For some reason the planes that were still undamaged didn't come after us. Maybe the aircraft we destroyed had blocked the runway and prevented them from taking off.

The ground rose up towards a plateau and the temperature dropped. There was not much of a track and we had to work our way up the rough boulder-strewn slopes as best we could. There was desert at the top too; a petrified sea of sand and rock. We buried Plummer and Jackson up there. The view was wonderful. You could see the sun come up in the morning and go down at night. What better place to put your bones down for good?

That evening I thought about Mary-Anne but when I tried to picture her I soon gave up. She seemed so remote, so inaccessible, and that last meeting of ours seemed more like a dream. I fell asleep, not thinking of Mary-Anne, then, but of Plummer, the cheerful Cockney, and Jackson that old sweat who had seemed so indestructible. Jackson had always been a bit of a mystery. Now he would never find that Paul Reynolds he'd been looking for. A pity.

We had received quite a knock. We lost a total of seven men, the two 2-tonners and a 15-hundredweight truck. The only transport left was the remaining 15-hundredweight and the two armoured cars. Our biggest asset, the twenty-five pounder, looked like a write-off. Frankly, I couldn't see us playing around with it in spite of what Long Tom said. Without wheels or open sights the thing would still fire but it would be a lethal hunk of metal in any situation.

At dawn a strong sand-laden wind was blowing and it was impossible to sit in an open vehicle without goggles. The sandstorm grew worse but we kept going because of the cover it gave us from aircraft. Again the sand came into the vehicle. It built up on the floor of the cab so that Butt, who was driving, had to kick it away from the accelerator pedal.

We found our way by compass as one does at sea. War in the desert is like war at sea. In both cases the opposing forces search and destroy. Nobody is interested in occupying a stretch of sea, or desert. The desert, like the sea, is merely the hunting ground and it is all a question of finding and destroying the enemy there.

Agedabiya consisted of a few tumble-down hovels, a cluster of palm trees and a muddy well used by camels, donkeys and men. There was also that petrol dump Rommel put there for his big push eastward. One evening we crept up close to take a look at it. We could tell by the way the ground was disturbed that there were mines and booby traps everywhere.

Barbed-wire entanglements ten-foot high surrounded the dump, and it was also well camouflaged from the air.

'I wouldn't be surprised if they had a battalion of crack troops guarding that place,' Long Tom told us after we crept back to the shelter of some rocks. 'It's vital we destroy that dump. If we cut our way through that wire and set off the alarm we'd be sitting ducks. Out in the open down there we wouldn't stand a chance. We'll have to use the twenty-five pounder.'

'That gun is just a load of scrap!'

'It will do one more job for us. If we can lob one or two shells into that dump there's a good chance the lot'll go up!'

Keeping well out of sight of the dump we brought up what was left of the gun and set it up by sighting through the barrel and using stones to raise or lower the elevation. Meanwhile, Long Tom and his men took up position behind some rocks with machine guns. When we were ready I tied a long piece of string to the firing mechanism of the gun and ordered everybody to take cover.

'Fire!'

The gun leapt back in a shower of dust and stones and fell over on to its side. The shell crashed into the petrol dump but missed the petrol.

'Take post!'

Men came running out of the buildings and a siren wailed as we righted the gun and set it up again for another round. We were in full view of the Germans, the smoke from our gun hanging like a small cloud over our position, and I knew that any minute now we would be at the receiving end of a hail of fire.

'Elevation up a little. Bearing three degrees right.'

We adjusted the stones. It was like preparing some ancient artillery piece for action.

'Ready!'

'Take cover!'

I gave a tug at the lanyard and ducked away. The shell screamed into the dump and burst among some huts. Before us lay thousands of gallons of petrol and so far not a tin was damaged! Rifle and machine-gun fire was coming at us now, the bullets whining and chipping off chunks of rock and then some sixth sense told me that they had an 88 down there.

'Take cover!'

But it was too late. Those 88 shells travel faster than sound and that first shell was a direct hit on our position. Four of Long Tom's men manning a machine gun simply disappeared. Almost immediately another shell hit Long Tom's armoured car and left it wrecked and smoking. The 88 had got the range and we wanted to get out of there but Long Tom, who was unhurt, stopped us. 'Third time lucky!'

This time what was left of our twenty-five pounder jumped up and almost brained us when it fired, but the shell burst amongst the densely-packed petrol tins in the middle of the dump and lightning flashes raced across the tins. The dump went up like a volcano and the explosion almost blew us off that hilltop. Hundreds of petrol cans soared into the sky and burst into flames like monstrous fire crackers. We abandoned our positions and ran for it. We didn't want to be around when that lot came down!

We drove deep into the desert but a Messerschmitt soon found us. The plane came out of the sun so low and fast that we could only duck. Butt was in the back of our truck and that first burst practically cut him in half. Three of Long Tom's men were killed too, and the remaining armoured car was set on fire. Long Tom, with a couple of men, rushed in to try and salvage some petrol cans. I knew why. We still had a 15-hundredweight truck and our road lay through an eternity of sand where just a cupful of water could be measured by the reading on the fuel gauge.

When the plane came round again we opened up with everything we had and Long Tom even emptied his pistol into it. The plane came round for a third run and this time, probably out of bravado, the pilot made his approach almost at ground level. We ducked as he roared overhead but his wing clipped the radio mast of our 15-hundredweight and he spun across the desert like a kid's paper plane and crashed in a pall of black smoke.

All I had now out of my original team of six was McAlister, Buckley and Corbett. Long Tom had fared badly too with only eight men left out of twenty. Altogether, now, we added up to twelve men. We had lost two 2-tonners, two armoured cars and a 15-hundredweight truck. If we hadn't got the other 15-hundredweight we'd have had to foot slog it back to base'.

We buried Butt and the three LRDG men and made crosses out of some bits and pieces of metal from wrecked vehicles. The ground was hard with shifting sand and a long way from the caravan routes. It was a lonely place and I wondered whether anybody would come across it, and if they did, would they ever guess what happened there?

The evening was hot and still and I was exhausted but couldn't sleep. Somehow, I had petrol on the brain. Petrol can keep an army on the move and it can get you to the next water hole. Yet what a wastage of the stuff there is! Men splash huge quantities of it around. They use it to start a fire when they're cold. They pour it on the sand to light their cooking fires. They burn out their refuse dumps and latrines with it and they use gallons of the stuff to wash out their overalls. If Rommel had half the petrol we sloshed about he'd have taken Cairo long ago.

I sat up suddenly. The air was heavy with the smell of petrol. The sentry was wandering about and I could see the glow of our fire. I got up to investigate and discovered that the 15-hundredweight was reeking of petrol so I stamped out the fire and hurried to rouse the others. Apparently several of the petrol cans had been pierced by minute slivers of shrapnel from that 88mm and our precious reserves were steadily dripping away. We saved what we could but it spoilt the rest of the night for us when we realized how close we came to being blown sky high if a spark from our camp fire drifted across to the truck.

Next day we headed south-eastward. It was so hot you could tip your tinned sausages out on to the bonnet of the truck and watch them sizzle.

'It's three hundred miles to Siwa,' Long Tom said. 'As things stand now, it'll be touch and go!'

There were now twelve of us on board and that 15-hundredweight truck would certainly drink up the fuel. Three hundred miles may not be all that far but when you have to negotiate the Great Libyan Plateau and then head out across a waterless sand sea it can seem more like a thousand. Water was the main problem. In that heat the truck needed more water than we did so we cut the water ration and saved what urine we had for the radiator.

Sometimes when we were miles from anywhere we would sit round our little fire and chat and one evening Long Tom told us about one of his earlier expeditions. It was December 1940. The British had launched an offensive and the Italian army, then a mighty force in North Africa, was in retreat. One of his jobs had been to swing round and harass the enemy columns from the rear. It had seemed a tall order for the LRDG but it had all been part of the British Army's strategy at the time and other units had been involved in the same operation. These hit-and-run tactics caused great confusion among the enemy who believed that the British had broken through at several different points.

'We had an Australian with us whom we called 'Tiger'. I really don't know why. Maybe it was because he had greenish coloured eyes and liked to grow his hair long and skip the odd shave. He was a little wild though and I often had to restrain him from getting up to foolhardy things. However, I couldn't keep my eyes on him all the time.'

Long Tom told us how they had driven the-Italians out of one of their forts.

'I'll never forget the booty we found. The Italians liked to ship out all the little luxuries of life – even to their remote outposts. There was tinned chicken, tinned ham, all kinds of delicious cheeses and wine, port and a brandy which could only have been matured in paradise. We had a party which the Italians tried to gate-crash but we fought them off. When they came at us with tanks the next day we really believed they wanted to get some of that stuff back – especially the brandy! Anyway, before I could stop him, Tiger grabbed our only sack of grenades and went out there on his own to meet them. We gave him all the covering fire we could but our bullets just bounced off that armour like peas. Tiger jumped on to the leading tank, pulled open the hatch and dropped a grenade into the control room. A quick thinking crewman picked it up and tossed it back outside. The explosion blew Tiger off the tank but by some miracle he was unhurt. He ran after the tank, climbed on board again, and dropped another grenade inside. This time he was on the hatch cover and counted to three before he jumped off.

That tank was a write-off. Not content with that he put another tank out of action by blowing off its tracks. He ran up close and dropped a grenade into the caterpillar mechanism. That crazy Australian used up our precious bombs but I don't think we could have done better ourselves!'

'What happened to Tiger?'

'Oh, we lost him.'

'Killed in action?'

'Good Lord, no! The Eyeties drove us into the desert. We had a fifteen hundredweight then, too, but that didn't help. We were down to less water than would fill an egg-cup and we'd just about had it when the Bedouin turned up. A whole village on the move. We traded our truck for water and a passage to wherever they were going. It was that or die of thirst. The Arabs don't give you anything for nothing!'

Long Tom laughed. 'It turned out to be Lake Chad, about a thousand miles to the south of us. They hitched our wagon to a camel and gave us all the water we could drink!'

'And Tiger?'

'We stayed with that caravan for a long time. Tiger got on well with the Arabs. You know how gorgeous some of those Arab girls can be? Well, he fell in love with one of them and she was only fifteen. When he asked the headman if he could marry her, he said yes, providing he renounced his Christian faith and became a Muslim. Tiger was not exactly a church-going man, so for him it was easy. He had already learned a little Arabic so he became a Muslim and married this Arab girl. I suppose I was what you would call best man. As for the rest of us, we met up with some Free French down at Fort Lamy and when they had a plane to spare going our way, they flew us back to Egypt.'

'What about Tiger, though, his home and family for instance and what about the army?'

'He hadn't much of a home. His mother was dead and his father drank too much. He stayed with the Arabs. He was happy that way.'

'But what about army records and all that? Wasn't he put down as a deserter?'

'No. Not by me anyway. Old Tiger did more for the war effort than most people and in my book he earned the VC twice over. I just told them he was missing, believed killed!'

'Do you think he's still with them?'

Long Tom grinned and nodded. 'Tiger Tiger burning bright, it was love for him at first sight! And judging how gorgeous that Arab girl was, he's probably got about ten kids by now!'

Halfway to Siwa the engine seized up and we broke down finally. We radioed for help and eventually a truck came out from the oasis to pick us up. By that time we were pretty thirsty. After a couple of days in Siwa we were flown back to Mersa Matruh. It was now the beginning of October and I had been away from my unit for over two months. Out of the twenty-seven men who started out, fifteen were killed. And we lost all six of our vehicles. Operation BOOMERANG was successful but expensive.

Buckley and McAlister were both restless types and now they wanted a transfer to the field artillery. They wanted to join my own unit.

'Alright, we've had a go with the LRDG,' the Australian said, 'and you've given us a pretty good training as field gunners. We'd like to join your crowd.'

I was flattered but a little sceptical. More often than not your application for a transfer in the army would be refused. On the other hand I could have a word with the 'powers that be'. After all, those two men had proved themselves to be very capable in some pretty tight spots. Great if I could get them into my own gun team.

'I should think well about it,' I warned them. 'Life with our kind of gun is not exactly a bed of roses. We've got twenty-five pounders, don't forget, and they put us right up in the muck and we're often in front of the infantry'.'

The sheep farmer screwed his weather-beaten face into a grin. 'Sounds fair dinkum. Anything for a lark, mate'.'

'How about you, Jock?'

'Och aye,' McAlister grunted. He was more bored than anything, I think, and he wanted a change. He shrugged. 'What the hell!'

I told them to apply in writing and I promised to have a word with the CO on my return. We had a farewell party the next day and I said goodbye to Long Tom.

'What are you going to do?' I asked him.

'Have a spot of leave.'

'Same here, maybe we'll meet up some place.'

There were all kinds of things I wanted to say but I didn't. He had lost fifteen of his men in Operation BOOMERANG and I could tell, somehow, that he still hadn't got around to writing all those letters.

He shook hands with me. 'Thanks for your help,' he said.

CHAPTER FIVE

The situation in North Africa was changing rapidly. The Germans were pouring in more troops, guns and tanks and they were also building up their air force. We, of course, were doing the same but, whereas our troops had to be sent all the way round the Cape, the Germans had only to cross from Messina in Sicily to Tripoli. The Germans were also able to provide their convoys with strong fighter protection from their air bases in Crete and Sicily. Nevertheless, this short sea passage was often a death trap and many of their transports were torpedoed and sunk by the Royal Navy. It has been said that on the bed of this stretch of water alone, between Messina and Tripoli, lie more troops than were ever killed in action in North Africa and more arms and equipment than the enemy forces ever used there. Now, in early October, two mighty armies stood facing each other across a tract of land more than twice the size of Europe, and there was every indication that both sides were preparing for a big offensive in the early winter.

I hitched a lift back to the front in a Bren-gun carrier. The driver told me that the British garrison at Tobruk was still holding out. Apparently he spent over three months in the besieged fortress himself before being relieved. The Germans had shelled and dive-bombed the town almost to rubble, he said. The troops who lined the thirty-five mile perimeter existed in the shallow trenches and dugouts which they had scraped out of the shelled and bomb-blasted earth. Out in front, only a short distance beyond the minefields and barbed-wire entanglements, lay the crack assault regiments of the German army.

The defenders of Tobruk had been under siege for months. They had been shelled, bombed and attacked by tanks and infantry but they still managed to cling on to that vital perimeter. The Germans were determined to capture the town because a victory here would release a large number of their best troops which would then be sent to reinforce their main army which was battling it out with the British about a hundred miles to the east.

Reinforcements and food and equipment could only be brought into the perimeter by night. The driver described the din of artillery, the crash of exploding shells and the great pall of smoke which hung perpetually over the town.

At night ships of the Royal Navy and Merchant Navy, often under aerial bombardment, had to creep past the partly-submerged wrecks in the harbour before unloading their cargoes of men and supplies. They would then take on the wounded and those men due to be relieved and slip away back to Mersa Matruh or Alexandria as quickly as possible. From what the man told me I got the impression that the 'Rats of Tobruk' were writing a pretty good chapter for themselves in the pages of history.

My unit had moved on to a different location, of course, but I found them eventually. There was a letter from Mary-Anne nearly two months old. She had been sent to work at a hospital near Sidi Batani. It looked as if they were getting the forward hospitals ready for the next push. If I'd known I could have looked in on her on the way up from Mersa.

The Colonel was impressed with what I had been doing and we had a discussion about Operation BOOMERANG.

'I am in two minds whether to keep you with us or send you off on an Officers' Training Course.'

'I would rather stay up here, sir.'

'You'd go down to Cairo and come away with a couple of pips on your shoulder. Wouldn't you like that? Think of the prospects. It could change your whole life…'

I hesitated. I had had an opportunity to apply for a commission before but turned it down. I was always a bit of a loner and I was not so sure I would be happy in an officers' mess. Besides I would have to say goodbye to all my friends. No. For me, Sergeant was the best rank. They could stuff their commission. I thanked him and asked if, instead, he could see his way to granting me a small favour.

'I was just trying to do you a favour,' he grumbled.

I told him about Buckley and McAlister and how well they had fought with the LRDG. 'They would like to come up here and join us, sir. They'd be good men to have in the Battery.'

'Good men, eh?' They're with the LRDG at Mersa?'

The Colonel scribbled on his pad. 'Right I'll see what I can do.'

I was about to leave but he stopped me.

'By the way, Sergeant, I've got some bad news for you. Two of your men were killed near here. It was about two weeks ago. Banks and Wainwright...'

He went on talking but I wasn't listening. Banks and Wainwright. And after all we had been through Rod, my Number Two, was dead.

'How did it happen, sir?'

'It was one of those damned minefields. Everybody thought the engineers had cleared it.'

I swore. Blown to pieces on some lousy minefield. Those two men deserved better than that!

'You've chalked up some leave for yourself. Ten days starting tomorrow. Pick up your pass from the Battery Commander's office...'

I stood there feeling numb, hoping that he had made a mistake. There was a big pile of papers on his desk. It looked as if he was going to be busy. He started to flip through them idly and then he looked up at me.

'Come to think of it, Sergeant, we shall need a couple of replacements. If those LRDG men of yours do come up here we might even put them in with your team.'

He was trying to soften the blow but I didn't want anybody else, not even Buckley and McAlister at the expense of those two.

I got little sleep that night. The old spectres wouldn't go away. Banks the miner with his rough Yorkshire humour. Maybe if he hadn't got drunk when he enlisted he would still be a miner today. Rod Wainwright. He had wanted to marry Kate McDonald and take her home to England with him. An uneasy thought then struck me. Rod had not been the sort of man to talk about his girlfriends and I believe that I was the only person he confided in. Was Kate McDonald still ignorant of his death?

Mary-Anne had been transferred to a hospital at Sidi Barrani. Should I spend my leave with her there or go on down to Cairo and see Kate McDonald? I tried to weigh the thing up. Mary-Anne would be busy at the hospital all day and our only chance of getting together would be when she came off duty in the evening. Then again, Sidi Barrani was just a wayside halt, a watering place on the road to Tobruk, and nobody in their right mind would want to spend ten days of their precious leave in a dump like that.

Meanwhile I had a leave pass for Cairo and as Rod's friend and Number One I felt that it was my duty to go down there and see Kate as soon as possible. I fell asleep and after what seemed to be only a minute or two I was wide awake again. It was cold. A single star hung low like a barn lamp. I was exhausted but I lay awake because I knew that it would soon be 'stand to' at first light.

I checked with my crew that morning but nobody knew that Rod had a girlfriend in Cairo. So it didn't look as if anybody had told Kate the bad news. That settled it. Those two people had been in love together. I would have to go down there and tell her myself.

First, I went to see Rod's grave. It was a good hour's drive across the desert. There was just the usual pile of stones and a rough wooden cross. Banks was buried alongside him. I would have liked to put some flowers there. Instead, I found some more stones.

It turned out that Corbett and Rule were also due for leave again and for the second time that year we travelled down to Cairo together. The worst part of anybody's leave was that desert road. Pitted and broken by tanks and lorries, it seemed endless and the traffic jams and sandstorms soon made you wonder why anybody bothered to go all that way in the first place. This, and the realization of what I had to tell Kate McDonald, made it a particularly miserable journey as far as I was concerned. We arrived in Cairo exhausted and filthy. Rule went off to his Salvation Army hostel, Corbett went off to some mysterious haunt of his own and I went straight to the Tipperary Club.

Most of the men there were just out from England. Their uniforms were clean and well-pressed, their boots polished. Young, fresh-faced, they looked startingly pale. The Tipperary Club was full of them. I stared at them and they stared at me. My clothes were crumpled and stained and my hair was coarse and matted and when I ran my hand through it the sand fell off on to the carpet. One of the soldiers was playing a piano. He looked as rough and tough as they come but he played beautifully. I had seen this before in the army and it was always a source of wonder to me how gifted those rough types can be. I noticed that the woman behind the counter was English, maybe it was because I hadn't seen a woman for months but I found myself staring at her. She was slim and dark and lovely to look at. She was probably in her forties, but then older women are often more attractive. This one, I decided with regret, was sure to be married.

The long journey had taken it out of me and I decided to see Kate the following day. I needed a good sleep. Come to think of it I hadn't slept in a bed since I was last in Cairo. I poured myself a large whisky and then I wallowed in a hot bath. And after that I had the best meal I'd had in months.

But I couldn't sleep. The same old faces slid by me: Long Tom, 'Daddy Bill' Jackson, Butt, Plummer, Banks and Wainwright and, of course, Mary-Anne. I tried to think about that woman in the Tipperary Club but the problem of Kate McDonald wouldn't go away. How could I possibly tell her that Rod was dead? Somehow, as I tossed and turned, the job seemed impossible. And then I remembered that I could always take a stiff drink. I clung to this idea and I believe it calmed me in the end and helped me to drop off.

When I called at the hospital the next day I discovered that Kate McDonald was still working there and that she would be coming off duty at midday. I decided that it would be best to speak to her outside the building and chose a bench where I had a good view of the main entrance and waited for her there. I had some whisky with me but I didn't drink any even when the clock struck twelve. I decided that I would walk up to her and tell her that Rod was dead, that he died bravely whilst in action against the enemy, and get the thing over just like that.

It was a full ten minutes before some people came out and then I recognized her almost at once. She looked slim and attractive in her nurse's uniform and I liked the way she had put her hair up into plaits and for a wild moment temptation stirred inside me. I'd tell her about Rod first and then I'd ask her if she'd join me for an evening meal at one of the restaurants. Maybe I should get to know her. After all, I still had most of my leave in front of me and it would be good to spend some of it with a pretty girl like this.

I was about to go up and speak to her when a man in uniform, probably one of the army doctors, beat me to it. I watched them as they stood chatting together and then, before I could do anything, they walked off down the drive and out of the main gates. I had nothing else to do so, I followed them. Maybe I would still get a chance to speak to her and, anyway, I was a little curious about her companion. Was he just a friend from the hospital or possibly a relation?

I followed them to a little chalet in the suburbs. There was bougainvillea in the garden and I could see the Nile beyond. I watched them as they stood there on the porch locked in each other's arms. Next minute they went inside. The front door slammed and I heard the girl's wild laughter. I felt a little bitter, then, for wanting to take her out myself and I cursed because I had wasted a whole day of my precious leave.

The days slid by and I wandered about Cairo. I went to the air-conditioned Metro cinema and visited the New Zealand club. I made a lot of friends whom I knew I would never see again. Most of all I enjoyed the sand-free food, the ice-cold drinks and a real bed at night. I did wonder about cutting my time in Cairo short and spending a day or two in Sidi Barrani on the way back but in the end I ruled it out. Mary-Anne was still in my thoughts of course but, somehow, so much had happened since I had last seen her that I began to wonder whether I was not just in love with the idea of being in love with her.

Corbett, Rule and I would meet in the New Zealand Club occasionally and I encouraged this plan because I wanted to keep an eye on Corbett. He was such a wild character that I wouldn't put it past him to get drunk and do a bunk or something silly. Anyway, next time I looked into the club I found him there much to my relief. He had been drinking a lot but what surprised me was that Rule, the strict non-alcoholic Salvation Army man, had been drinking too, and I cursed Corbett for being such a bad influence on him and leading him astray like that.

Corbett's big round face was grinning happily as he held up his glass. 'Rule here decided it was time he broke his rule. After all, a glass or two of beer never harmed anyone!'

I could see they'd both had more than that. They'd probably had a few chasers too.

'Not if they weren't teetotal. Start a man off on alcohol out here and there'll be no end to it. Why didn't you leave him alone?'

Rule looked up at me with a stupid grin on his normally grave face.

'Don't blame him. I was thirsty so he gave me a sip of his beer. It was lovely stuff so I thought I'd have a glass or two. Anyway, why don't you mind your own business and f…. off.'

I had never heard Rule swear let alone use such a dreadful word but I let it pass and I ordered a drink from the waiter. I needed it!

'There you go. You're having a drink yourself and you're supposed to set us an example being our Number One!'

Rule drained his glass and banged it down on the table.

Corbett winked at me. 'He's going to have more than a glass of beer before this night's out!'

'What do you mean?'

'Tom and I are off to the Birka.'

I wasn't all that surprised. The desert had obviously proved too much for the staid little Welshman. Well, it had happened before.

'No, you're not. I'm your Number One and I'm telling you[1].'

'Yeah?' Corbett leered. 'You can't stop us. We got our rights and you know it. The Birka's not out of bounds!'

I knew that there had been a movement to shut down the brothels but the Birka, at any rate, was still in business.

I knew, too, that if I said any more I'd have a fight on my hands with Corbett. A sergeant fighting a gunner? If the MPs came in on it I would be busted. So I said nothing and enjoyed my drink. Afterwards I would follow them both and try and prevent Rule from losing all that he had been living up to. Corbett, who spent much of his time in the brothels anyway, could go to hell!

It was a long wait. Corbett insisted on buying me another round and if I refused to accept it he would have taken it as an insult. Then, of course, it was my turn, and then Rule's and when we finally staggered out of that place it was past midnight. I let Corbett and Rule go on ahead while I followed a short distance behind. I had been hoping that Corbett would have changed his mind about the Birka, particularly as it was so late, but not a bit of it. He strode on purposefully and knew exactly where to go.

Cairo had its smells but the Birka had a smell of its own and this can best be described as a mixture of a heady perfume, garlic, blocked sewers and horse droppings. Most of the girls standing about there managed to look quite lovely but a closer look made me realize that this loveliness was merely the thickness of a coat of paint.

By now, Corbett, not caring about Rule anymore, had gone on ahead and I saw my chance. If Rule couldn't save his own soul then it was up to his Number One to try and save it for him. I caught up with him and swung him round but he struggled free and I thought he was going to hit me. If you've ever tried to stop a man from having his sex you'll know what I mean. I could have sworn that Welshman would have done for me had he half the chance. He swore at me and then he turned round and crossed the road and followed one of those beckoning beauties into her house.

What should I do? Rule was a grown man; furthermore he was a soldier, so who was I to interfere with his rights? The brothels were supposed to be medically inspected so maybe I should let him have his fun. Besides, if I had gone in there and dragged him out I could have been in real trouble. There were plenty of layabout soldiers in there who would have been only too glad to get a sergeant into trouble by being witnesses to such an assault, so in the end I left him there.

I had a lot to drink and I was tired and of course tempted, too, when a beautiful girl clad in a tightly fitting satin sheath of a dress beckoned to me. I could smell her perfume from across the street and she smiled at me when I went up to her. She looked so clean and gorgeous she might have been a model in one of those Bond Street fashion houses. She entered a dingy double-storey dwelling house and pulled a brightly coloured curtain aside. The sudden light made me blink but when I got used to it I could see soldiers in there, among them Corbett with his bloated face and happy grin, and somehow that and the smell was like a punch in the guts.

The Salvation Army get around. You can find them in any dismal city street, in any murky port or dockside in the world. I had even seen them in the desert. That evening they were in Cairo and their band was playing 'Take my Life and Let it Be!'

CHAPTER SIX

The dawn of 17 November brought a cold hard rain which even the desert could not soak up. At night it was pitch black and we tried to shelter beneath our vehicles but the water ran across the ground and soaked us in our groundsheets. We tried to sleep in the back of our truck but the rain came under the tarpaulin and flooded the floor.

Buckley and McAlister had got their transfer and now joined our gun team. Corbett, Rule, Walton and myself made up the detachment of six men. Our Battery waited in the pouring rain, its guns and limbers hooked up. Sometime in the early hours of the morning we would move off. Tomorrow, the biggest offensive yet, an all-out attempt to relieve Tobruk and destroy the Axis forces in North Africa, was due to be launched. The British were ready with about 120,000 men and 900 tanks. The Axis had about 140,000 men and 500 tanks. Tomorrow would see the beginning of a mighty struggle not for the mastery of the desert but for the future of the African continent itself.

We knew the enemy, too, were ready to launch an offensive and, according to intelligence reports, their attack was believed to be planned for 24 November. They intended to push us back into Egypt and take the Suez Canal but one of their main objectives was to remove once and for all that thorn in their flesh – Tobruk.

During that endless downpour, while the rain turned the desert into a thick sticky morass, while everybody was shivering and trying to keep warm, nobody on the enemy side dreamed that the British would attack first.

And it was at the little village of Beda Littoria far behind the Axis lines on the Cyrenaican coast, that the ill-fated attempt to capture Rommel took place. A party of British commandos landed there at night from a submarine. The seas were so rough that only a small number of men managed to get ashore. On 17 November they assembled in the pitch darkness close to where they believed Rommel had his headquarters. If they couldn't capture him they were to kill him in the hope that this would create panic on the very eve of the British offensive so that when the attack came the Panzerarmee would be without their Commander in Chief. As it turned out Rommel was not in Beda Littoria that evening. In short, the operation was a bloody shambles with most of the British commandos being killed or captured.

The rain flooded the ground, filled the hollows, and poured into the wadis until the troops sheltering there had to get out or lose all their equipment and in some places were even in danger of drowning. The time and the date had been fixed and nothing, not even the rain, could stop us. The Royal Navy, which dominated the coast between Alexandria and Tobruk, was ready with its tremendous firepower. Behind us, the squadrons of Hurricanes and Blenheim bombers were beginning to warm up their engines.

The troops which were to take part in the attack were XXX Corps which included the 7th Armoured Division – the Division which had as its sign the Jerboa, or desert rat – and to which I also belonged. And there was the 1st South African Division and 22 Guards Brigade. These formations were to attack from Maddalena in the south. The 2nd New Zealand Division and the 4th Indian Division would strike up north by the coast.

Soon after midnight the rain-sodden night was blasted by hundreds of engines as this tremendous armada moved forward. During the First World War men had risen from the trenches and gone over the top. We, too, had, I suppose, gone over the top now. The only difference was that we had no trenches to fall back into if things went wrong.

We had to fight our battles in the open desert and if we lost we were hunted down and there was no place to hide. Furthermore, we, the field artillery, had to get our guns in much closer to the enemy then they ever did in that previous war. And only too often we had no choice but to stay put and blast away out there while the German armour did their best to run us down.

We were tired and soaked but we were part of an immense army on the move and I think most of us found it exhilarating. I could hear laughter, even singing, and men opened up their little hoards of looted alcohol and smoked their best cigarettes.

Suddenly ahead, the crash of gunfire, the flashes ripping across the night sky like the beating of titanic wings. The first tanks had met. Tubby Wilson, leading our column, stopped his car and waved us down. He called the Number Ones for a briefing. We huddled round him while he shone his torch on the rain-soaked map.

'As you know, we are supporting the 11th Hussars and their tanks are right out there in front of us. The idea is to break through the enemy line here and then head north for Tobruk.' He waved towards a shallow wadi which was lit by the flash of gunfire, 'Get your guns into position over there but be ready to move out quickly!'

We were not supposed to smoke or light any fires but we were old hands at doing what we wanted to do and after we had unloaded the ammunition we lit a small fire in a hacked-out petrol tin and brewed some strong tea. We even managed to heat up a few tins of bully beef. The rain had eased a little and, as we warmed ourselves by the fire, we enjoyed our breakfast. As the light grew stronger we could see our other three guns spaced out on our left-hand side. The signal lines had been laid in record time and we were ready for action.

I had just about the best team ever. Buckley, McAlister and Corbett actually seemed to be enjoying themselves although I had to keep an eye on them because they were tipping whisky into their tea. At present, Doug Walton was doing the job of layer while Rule handled the elevation but all six of us could do the same job of course. The morning was cold, wet and miserable. Out in front of us the rumbling and thumping of the tank battle went on like the sound of some monstrous landslide, but there was nothing we could do until both sides disengaged because if we opened fire now we would hit our own tanks. For once we had plenty of water so we could wash ourselves and dig out some dry clothes while we had the chance. Seven o'clock and still no orders had come down for us to engage any targets and I wondered what on earth was happening.

'We seem to be knocking hell out of them by the sound of it!' Walton exclaimed.

'Maybe all that noise is what they're doing to us!' Corbett said.

Buckley fished out a cigarette. 'What do you think of our chances Sarge?'

'Frankly, I think our latest general has made a big mistake. I've seen the plan of attack. They've split the army up into three separate spearheads. Down here, in the middle and up north by the sea. That's exactly what Rommel wants and if we don't look out he'll be up to his old tricks again and he'll go round each of those army units and destroy them all piecemeal!'

'Pity old Wavell had to go,' Walton muttered.

I agreed. 'He was a great general. He carved up the Italians long before Rommel came on the scene. In those days he had about 30,000 men and the Italians, under Graziani, had more than 300,000. Wavell did it all by employing the same tactics that Rommel uses today!'

'Why on earth did he have to go? He'll be wasted in India!'

'They slung Wavell out because he couldn't stop the Germans when they pushed us back last summer. That, and he couldn't relieve Tobruk. Everybody had forgotten how he wiped the floor with the Italian army!'

'But that was crazy. Wavell was a brilliant general,' said Walton. 'He was really one of us. He'd have a mug of tea and share a tin of bully beef with you. You could talk to him.'

I knew all that only too well. 'We get rid of our generals if they don't win battles,' I said. 'We're too strait laced and old fashioned in this army. If Rommel had been in charge of us instead of Wavell we'd probably have booted him out too. Rommel has made one or two bloomers like Wavell and he can lose the odd battle but the Germans don't get rid of him. He's still there right on top because the Germans know when they've got a good man.' Sergeant Major Palmer suddenly appeared out of the murk. 'You'll get shot if anybody sees that fire of yours. You know the orders. Got some tea by the way?'

I poured him a strong mugful and put in plenty of milk and sugar. 'Sergeant Major's cup of tea!'

He stood there, tall and lean, his cold eyes taking in every detail of our gun position. Then he pointed to our little pile of wet and dirty shells.

'Clean 'em up unless you want to go to hell before your time!'

I tried to divert his attention. 'What's going on, sir? Why haven't we found any targets?'

He finished his tea and I poured him another. 'What's up? It's nice and quiet here. You asking for trouble? Look here Sergeant, this is one hell of a business. You hear that racket? We've just got to wait here until those tanks have busted themselves up. If we win then it's up stakes and we can admire the scenery again. If they win they'll be coming through here like a load of shit!' He nodded at Buckley and McAlister. 'I see you've got your replacements.' 'Buckley here is from Australia, sir. McAlister is from Glasgow. They were both in the Long Range Desert Group.'

'Couple of gangsters, eh? Well, maybe it's time we had something like that up here!' He handed me back his mug. 'There's one thing, Sergeant, that'll maybe get you through those Pearly Gates. You know how to make a cup of tea!' Palmer had gone across to Number Two gun when an 88 started shelling us. We hadn't dug any slit trenches, so we took what cover we could and I found myself sheltering behind our little stack of 25-pounder shells. Even that small pile of high explosive seemed better than nothing. It was uncanny how the 88 got on to us but those guns always did bring us bad luck. A number of our vehicles were racing about trying to get clear and I envied the drivers and anybody who managed to get a lift. As a gunner you sometimes feel isolated. You can't just clear off like the infantry. You've got to stay put whatever's happening until some transport arrives to pull you out. If you were likely to be over-run or captured you were supposed to smash the breech block or take it out and bury it in the sand. You were not nearly as mobile as the infantry because you had a 25-pounder field gun round your neck.

'Take post!'

The tannoy was blaring suddenly. The Battery was to engage enemy tanks and we were to use armour-piercing cap. We struggled to our feet as the range and angle to be put on the gun came over on the loudspeaker. The 88 shells were coming over with that high velocity scream and bursting close by, the pieces of metal humming and pinging like angry hornets as we took our positions on the gun. We had forgotten to put our tins hats on, not that they were any good, but they made you feel better. Sometime during the night Doug Walton had padded himself out with books and magazines and now these worked themselves loose and fell about all over the place.

'Fire!'

The gun leapt and the flash seemed to freeze the crew into white spectre-like figures beneath the billowing camouflage netting. The blast was worse than usual and I put it down to the heavy rain-sodden atmosphere. The smoke, too, hung about and choked us with its reek of cordite.

The corrections kept coming in over the tannoy. The enemy were bringing up huge concentrations of tanks, self-propelled guns and infantry formations and we fired almost continuously at various targets. But that 88 would not leave us alone. There were some casualties on the other guns and in the end we had to get out.

The trucks raced up but our own vehicle, partly loaded with 25-pounder ammunition, had been hit and the driver killed. The truck, out of control, ran across the desert until the petrol tank exploded. We watched it continue, an inferno, until all that ammunition blew it to smithereens. The other three guns pulled out in record time. The ammunition wagons then left, followed by the Battery Commander's car and the wireless truck and in the confusion nobody noticed that we had been left behind. We were alone in the desert and the 88 had us all to itself and, as if to emphasize the point, one of its shells burst close by and showered us with sand and stones. The morning was dark and heavy with clouds and the flash from that 88 could be clearly seen. We had nothing else to do until somebody discovered that we were missing, so we decided to have a go at it. We whipped the gun round, worked out an approximate range and commenced firing at something over 6,000 yards. The 88 fell silent. If we were not hitting them at least we were making them keep their heads down!

Buckley gave a sudden yell and, when we listened, we could hear the rumble of engines and the grinding of gears. Trucks, lorries, a convoy? British or German? It was always a question mark in the desert. And then we heard the squeal of tank tracks and the leading tank came out of the murk – that sinister silhouette which they had drummed into us at every training lecture – the German Mark IV.

'Tanks. Eleven o'clock. Open sights. Ten rounds gunfire. Fire'

The tanks, their guns swinging round on to us, spread out in line abreast and headed straight towards us. We had no time to think. We had plenty of ammunition piled up there and we worked like demons. The first shots from the Mark IVs were fired hurriedly and were too high but the wind from them almost knocked us over. However, firing point-blank as we were, it was easier for us to score a hit than it was for them to aim at a comparatively small target in their jolting heaving tanks. We hit three of those Mark IVs and the black smoke which poured out of them drifted across the others like a smokescreen and probably saved us. As luck would have it one of our 15-hundredweight trucks came racing up and got us out of the jam. Apparently the Battery Commander had discovered that we had been left behind and despatched the truck to pull us out. We were only just in time because those tanks had got the range and in another few minutes they would have blasted us off the desert.

The next few days were pretty chaotic. Sometimes we got the guns into position, off-loaded some ammunition, put the camouflage netting over them and dug slit trenches only to move out without firing a shot. Trucks and lorries of every description with all kinds of regimental, brigade or divisional signs were milling about everywhere and their drivers didn't know what to do or where to go. The desert was like some vast car park in which all the drivers had gone berserk. Isolated bands of men wandered about trying to find their units, and when I saw a staff car with red-tabbed officers standing about arguing over a map, I got the impression that the army was in a mess and that the big offensive had been a flop.

One morning we went into action at a place called Sidi Rezegh and as we dug our slit trenches the tanks thundered past us. It was hot and the crew including the commander sat on top. Only the driver was inside. The inside of a tank can become almost unbearably hot and providing they were not actually in action the crew would sit about on the tank outside. As we watched them go by we noticed that the sides of the tanks were strewn about with water bottles and cans, food canisters, petrol tins and spades and axes and other assorted equipment. There were even makeshift washing lines with towels, underwear and all kinds of clothing hanging out to dry. We cheered them on their way and Corbett pointed out the washing lines and made some remark about gypsies. But it was good to see them go by just as they must have been pleased, too, to see that they had some artillery to back them up. There is often a kind of mystique about tanks. If a tank appears in the streets people feel subdued. Well, here were dozens of the steel monsters!

'That lot'll churn out more bangers than a Berlin sausage factory!' Buckley remarked.

'Trouble is,' Corbett said, 'some of those Jerry tanks have got bigger guns than our twenty-five pounders and being self-propelled they can dodge about and manoeuvre and get out of trouble quickly. Us lot are sitting ducks right out in the open, with no inches – thick armour plating all round, and we can only get the hell out of it when our blasted trucks come up!'

'When you're out here, static, like us, you can aim better,' I said. 'It's difficult to hit anything when you're jolting about inside a tank. Besides, have you ever thought what it's like to be bottled up in a tank and you get a direct hit which touches off the petrol or ammunition, you can't get the hatch open and you're trapped in a steel oven? Give me the open air any day. Here at least you stand some sort of chance.'

We went forward again that evening. There was no moon but you could read a newspaper by the flash of gunfire. By the time we had unloaded the ammunition, dug slit trenches and put the camouflage netting over the gun it was past midnight. This time the order about no smoking or lighting fires really had to be enforced and we had also been warned to keep our voices down. The Germans, apparently, were all over the place and some of their transport had passed close enough during the night for us to hear them talking.

It was my turn for guard duty between 3 and 5 a.m. This was always the worst shift because you had to get what sleep you could before 3 a.m. and when you came off at 5 a.m. you would be lucky if you got your head down again. Sentry duty can be an eerie business especially at night. You never knew whether the enemy had any patrols about and the more you stared into the darkness the more you could swear that something moved. The time dragged and the same uneasy feeling was always there. Would some bloodthirsty patrol creep up on you and knife you in the back? It was always a relief to 'Take post' and shoot off a few rounds during those long dark hours.

But for me that three to five hour stint does have its compensation. There is always that moment when the last vestige of darkness dissolves and the world seems to hold its breath – when the sun rises blood red out of that sea of sand.

Today it was different. As the light spread, the desert showed its true colours and I counted eighteen German Mark IV tanks. They were only about 2,000 yards away and must have been sitting out there all night. I alerted the Command Post and the order came down for us to take post. The men cursed as they rolled out of their blankets. None of us were in any mood to take on tanks without that first precious mugful of strong tea.

The Mark IVs saw us, too, and lightning flashes ran across the desert and the shells threw up the sand in front of us like an oncoming tidal wave. Then they came straight for us, the dust streaming out behind them. We depressed the barrel and fired across open sights but we couldn't stop them. Unfortunately, the Battery had been short of armour-piercing shells and, therefore, all we had with us at that particular gun position was high explosive.

The leading tank headed directly for Number Two gun and the crew jumped away and ran for their lives. The tank went right over the gun and crushed it into a heap of unrecognizable junk. Another tank came straight for us but we smashed it off course with a direct hit. That tank still came on, however, and we scattered and all I could do was dive into my slit trench. As I lay there the grinding and roaring of the tank's engine became deafening and then the light went out and I found myself in pitch darkness. When the hot oil started to drip on to me and the suffocating exhaust fumes made me choke, I realized that the tank was sitting on top of my trench. The tank then began to swivel round on one of its tracks, pushing the sand and muck in on me. I had always believed in digging a fairly deep and narrow trench but it now looked as if I had dug my own grave! I was beginning to wonder whether being crushed to pulp would be a quick way to go when the tank, which could have bogged down in that trench and which was now, of course, a sitting target, moved on. It is incredible how heavy a little sand can be and it took all my strength to get out of that trench.

The rest of my crew were safe but our gun position was a mess. The Mark IV had driven straight into our pile of shells and scattered them all over the place. Many of them were torn and dented and it was a miracle that none had exploded. I was just in time to see the tank with our camouflage netting caught up on it disappear into the smoke behind us. Our gun seemed to be undamaged and as we started to sort out the still usable shells we saw the Red Cross wagon weaving about as it tried to dodge the still smoking shell holes.

We learned that two men on Number Two gun had been killed by machine-gun fire. Sergeant 'Paddy' O'Brien, the Number One, had a leg blown off and he had also been hit badly by shrapnel. He died, later, in the ambulance on the way to the Casualty Clearing Station. The layer on Number Three gun had the top of his head taken off, while the man next to him had his right arm blown away. Number Four gun had one man killed and two wounded by grenades which the Germans had tossed out of their tanks as they went past us.

'Tubby' Wilson, the Battery Commander, drove up. His clothes were torn and he was covered in dirt and oil and there was a wild look in his face I hadn't seen before.

'The whole line's gone to pot. Drop everything, we're pulling out!' He stood there staring at the twisted remains of Number Two gun, then when he saw the Red Cross wagon and the stretcher bearers he hurried across to them. Meanwhile our own truck came racing up and we hooked up the gun and loaded as many of the good shells as we could find. Wilson came back to us then and gave me a map reference.

'We rendezvous here. If anything goes wrong and nobody turns up you'd better turn round and drive south and then east until you meet up with our chaps.' He gave a stab at the map. 'Remember, if you go any farther west beyond this point you'll end up in the bag. The rest of the Battery are either on the way or will follow when we've sorted out this mess. Good luck!'

Soon after we left that position a convoy of trucks and lorries came towards us. We knew that the Germans made good use of their captured vehicles so we kept a wary eye on them. The drivers turned out to be British and when we tried to stop them they accelerated past us. 'Serve them right if they catch up with those tanks'.' Buckley said.

We came to a place where the desert was criss-crossed with tank tracks and littered with the burnt-out hulks of tanks, lorries and assorted transport. Nobody had buried the dead and as we drew close the vultures rose drunkenly. Soon more vehicles came racing towards us. Trucks, lorries, Bren-gun carriers, tank transporters, motorcyclists. Their Divisional signs were all mixed up and they drove wildly, spread out across the desert in what appeared to be an all-out race to see who could reach the Egyptian frontier first. We tried to stop them but they paid no attention to our signals and roared on past. Soon afterwards a motorized infantry detachment came towards us followed by a battery of 4.5-inch guns, then a squadron of tanks. Tanks travelling north eastwards – the direction we were not allowed to take!

An officer climbed out of his car and waved us down. 'Where is your regiment? Where do you think you're going? Why are you travelling westward?'

I told him we had orders to rendezvous at a certain map reference and I gave him the coordinates. He went across to his car and came back with his map case. The map of the area we were fighting in was already displayed neatly on top.

'According to the information I was given back at Headquarters the position to which those coordinates refer is now in enemy hands You'd better turn your gun round and follow me.' He pointed north-east. 'That's where you'll find your regiment now – if it still exists!' He climbed into his car and drove off.

'What should I do? I cursed because I should have asked him for his name and unit. And now he was speeding off to catch up with his men. We waited there, undecided, and once I saw him turn and stare at us. He was obviously wondering why we hadn't turned round. After consulting my crew I decided to keep going westward. It was always safer to go forward rather than back when you're in the front line. I had awful visions of being accused of retreating without orders and who would listen to me if I tried to explain that some unknown officer had told me to go north-east!

We had stopped for a brew-up when Tubby Wilson with numbers three and four guns and what was left of their crews, together with the ammunition lorries and wireless truck, turned up. I told him what the officer had said but Wilson insisted on proceeding to the map reference in question.

'I don't see any problem. We've still got three of our guns and if the Germans are over there we shall just have to take them on. Isn't that what it's all about?'

Well, who was I to question such infinite wisdom?

The Germans were there, of course, and they had already over-run that map reference. Their tanks and motorized infantry were pushing southwards through the desert in a pincer movement while farther north they were coming along the coast road. However, Tubby Wilson had, meanwhile, made contact with the rest of the regiment which had five of its guns left, so we came together as a last-ditch combat group to try and stop the Axis advance.

Then began a long series of actions. Advancing, retreating and getting lost in the chaos of an attack which had gone terribly wrong. It is almost impossible for the ordinary soldier to know what is going on outside his own particular sphere of battle and it was only afterwards that we learned that the 21st Panzer Division had tried to encircle us at Sidi Rezegh. There had been a big tank battle and we lost about 500 tanks. The Tobruk garrison tried to break out but only a few infantry tanks made it and the Germans were still holding out at Halfaya Pass.

The British Army's mistake had been to fight in bits and pieces with its forces scattered all over the place. Worse, one of its generals wanted to fall back and form a new line in Egypt. This officer had therefore been dismissed and another general put in command. This new man was determined to stop the retreat. The vital plan was to keep the Eighth Army intact and however far it fell back it should, at all cost, be kept together as a solid fighting formation and words such as 'to the last bullet' and 'victory or death' were meant literally.

The big news had been how Rommel had led the 21st Panzer Division in a headlong dash towards Madallena and Sidi Omar in an attempt to cut off the British Army, relieve Halfaya Pass and drive on to the Nile. Rommel was under the impression that the British forces facing Tobruk were in rout, but the commanding general had already stopped any retreat on that front. Rommel then came up against the reinforced 4th Indian Division and other troops. He ran short of petrol and supplies and could not make it to Halfaya so he turned north and attacked the New Zealanders. Eventually the 21st Panzer Division was pulled back to the Tobruk front. This, then, was the stage during those hectic closing weeks of 1941 in which we, the actors, were underpaid, underfed, under-privileged and under fire.

A warm wind from the tropical south had dried out the desert and taken the chill from the air and it was good to lie on the sand and stretch out. We were waiting there in a shallow wadi for new targets to engage and Corbett was sharing a bottle of Schnapps which he had taken from a wrecked German lorry. Life for the moment was good. It was probably against the rules to drink while you were manning a gun but nobody seemed to worry about that. After all, you were a long time dead.

And when you are lying on the warm sand with a bottle of booze what else is there to talk about except 'Subject Normal'? Corbett had been telling us about his leave in Cairo. He spoke in a hushed voice and a glazed look had come into his eyes.

'I fell in love with one of the girls I met there. She was gorgeous!'

'Oh yeah?' Buckley put in derisively. 'Been to the Birka again then?'

'I didn't meet her in the Birka,' Corbett protested angrily. 'She wouldn't even know where that place is. I'm talking about Isobella.'

We exchanged glances. Isobella? How could this rough Geordie know anybody with such a pretty name.

'I call her Bell for short. She has her own flat in Heliopolis. She's not married. She is just waiting for her one and only to come along. Her knight in shining armour…'

The Australian gave a short laugh. 'Meaning you I suppose?'

'Want to make something out of it?' Corbett asked belligerently.

I had to step in to try and calm his down. 'I thought you had a good friend in the Birka too. Let me see, what was her name again?'

'Clara?' Corbett nodded slowly. 'She was in a different class altogether, of course, but she was lovely too.' He grinned suddenly. 'When she was good she was very very good, when she was bad she was terrific! Mind you, just because she works in the Birka you mustn't think that's wrong. There are lots of nice clean girls down there. After all, one has to earn a living, and can you think of a nobler cause than sacrificing yourself for our gallant fighting men?'

At this Rule stirred uneasily. True, he had fallen by the wayside but so had that woman in the Bible. She had been forgiven readily enough and so, he hoped, had he. Furthermore, the realization that he had not contracted any dreadful disease bucked him up enormously. He could say that he was back to square one again; a good Salvation Army man who was better prepared than ever to help his fellow man and to prevent him from falling into a similar sin.

The tanks thundered by and the dust rose, blotting out the sun. We could tell by the blackened and dented armour plating that they had been in battle, and now they were going back into the cauldron, for they were heading north-west towards Rommel's 21st Panzer Division.

'I wouldn't like to be inside one of those things,' Rule said.

'Yeah, especially if you're hit by armour-piercing shells,' Buckley replied. 'I looked inside a tank once. One of those shells had ricocheted round inside the cabin and decapitated the entire crew!'

'Fire is the worst thing,' Corbett put in, 'especially if the hatch jams!'

'I saw a man fall right under the caterpillar tracks back there,' McAlister said, not to be outdone. 'Talk about jam roly poly!'

Walton told them to shut up. 'We were just having a nice little chat about women. How about you, Sarge? What about the Birka?'

'What about it?'

'I don't suppose he's ever been there,' Buckley said maliciously.

'I did look in there once. Frankly I'd sooner be up here when the Khamseen's blowing!'

Corbett gave a short laugh. 'I've been there lots of times and I'm fine.'

'How do you know? Sometimes you can't tell for months, years even.'

Rule shifted uneasily. He looked worried.

'Anybody who's been to the Birka should see the MO and have a check up even if those places are medically inspected.'

Corbett was not in the least bothered but the Welshman looked so miserable that I changed the subject. 'What's all this about ponies down the pit?'

'It's perfectly true. I told you before. They've had ponies down the pit for as long as coal has been mined. Those animals are indispensable. We look after them, mind you. They have to be strong and healthy.'

Rule told us something about his life in a Welsh mining village.

'My father was a miner and his father before him. We worked hard to bring the coal up – most of which was sent to England of course. You must understand the valleys to understand Wales. We were a close-knit community. We were hungry and poorly paid and our

Mark Carter, the Author, in uniform in 1939.

Two years later, with his knees brown, in the desert.

With his gun detachment in the desert, 1941. Lance Bombardier Carter is sitting on the left, holding a white mug.

King Farouk I of Egypt, with Queen Farida. Farouk was educated at the Royal Military Academy, Woolwich, where Royal Artillery and Royal Engineer officers were trained. Initially popular, his love of luxury led to his being deposed in 1952. Egypt remained neutral until 1943 when the treat from the Axis had passed. (9 HAA Archive)

Alexandria harbour from the air. The harbour was the eastern home of the Royal Navy's Mediterranean Fleet and was defended by the Royal Artillery. The city was also an attractive leave centre for troops who were serving in the desert. (9 HAA Archive)

The Sphinx and the Pyramids at Giza, another popular spot for troops on leave.
(9 HAA Archive)

One of the difficulties of life in the desert was the *khamsin* or sandstorm which would
blot out visibility completely. Sand could even find its way into a closed-down vehicle
and for those in the open there was no escape. (9 HAA Archive)

'Easy living' in the desert. These Gunners at Sidi Barrani in the summer of 1941 have constructed a makeshift shelter to protect them from the worst of the sun although it would have provided no shelter in a *khamsin*. (9 HAA Archive)

Italian graves at Sidi Barrani. These were the last resting places of Italian soldiers who had died in the Operation COMPASS battles of December 1940. (9 HAA Archive)

The enemy. A German Panzer Mk III with the Deutsches Afrikakorps' emblem, a palm tree, emblazoned on the hull. Although lightly armed and lightly armoured, the Mk III was mechanically much more reliable than most British tanks. (IWM: E2881)

The Panzer Mk IV, a more formidable opponent than the Mk III. This is the earlier version with a short-barrelled gun. (Courtesy; Bundesarchiv)

A Panzer Mk IV blazes after being it during the Operation CRUSADER battles of late-1941. A British Crusader tank passes by.

The Panzer IV was upgraded with a heavier gun and its armour was also improved. It remained the basic German tank until the end of the war. This example, in Deutsches Afrikakorps camouflage and with the DAK emblem, resides in the Deutsches Panzermuseum in Munster. (Courtesy, Deutsches Panzermuseum)

In the early phase of the desert war the best British tank was the Matilda II I-tank, or Infantry tank. Well armoured and reliable, the Matilda suffered from its low speed as it was intended to support infantry and its light armament, a 2-pounder gun. (IWM: E4961)

Another view of a Matilda, entangled in barbed wire. The size of the turret meant that a heavier gun could not be fitted. Even so, Matilda II remained in service until the end of the war, being adapted for a range of special duties. (IWM: E4969)

The other class of British tank was the Cruiser. These were fast moving but also lightly armed, with the 2-pounder. This is a Mk IV Cruiser, built by the Nuffield Organisation to take advantage of the American Christie suspension. However, it lacked mechanical reliability. (IWM: 2632)

The British Valentine I-tank was a much better tank than most of its British contemporaries but again suffered from the light armament of a 2-pounder gun. However, it was reliable and the Red Army appreciated Valentines supplied under Lend-Lease. (IWM: E9772)

Some tanks changed sides. This Matilda II was captured by the Germans and marked with a plethora of black crosses, presumably to protect it from its friends. (IWM: E7842)

Italian tank crews faced their foes in these Fiat Ansaldo Carro Armato 13/40 tanks. These lacked a heavy gun and were only lightly armoured and called for great courage on the part of the crews who were never found wanting. Some captured 13/40s were impressed into British service. (Courtesy, Bundesarchiv)

Lacking an anti-tank gun that could take on the German tanks on equal terms, British forces adapted their 25-pounder field guns to the anti-tank role. This is an early 25-pounder, known as an 18/25-pounder, in action in the desert. (IWM: E2615)

Two 18/25-pounders in action. (IWM: E2831)

Gun duel. A gun detachment returns fire. (Private collection)

A 25-pounder troop in action in the desert. The gunners are wearing battledress trousers and heavy wool shirts, indicating that the photograph was taken during the winter months. (IWM: E9535)

This shot was taken in the summer months as the detachment are wearing shorts or lightweight trousers. Note the wheel on which the 25-pounder could be traversed. (IWM: 4824)

Most of a battery lines up for a practice shoot. (IWM: E2573)

Ready for anything. A determined gun detachment pose for the camera. (IWM: E3424)

The advent of the 6-pounder anti-tank gun meant that the 25-pounders could be relieved of their anti-tank role as the new weapon was a much more effective counter to the German armour than the 2-pounder. (Private collection)

A 6-pounder detachment in action in the desert. The gun came as a shock to the German panzer crews. (Private collection)

Used 25-pounder ammunition boxes at El Alamein. No longer needed in the anti-tank role, the 25-pounder regiments could play a greater part in the punishment of the Axis ground forces. (Private collection)

On the road to Tripoli. British troops passed through L'Arco dei Fileni, known to them as Mussolini's 'Marble Arch', which marked the boundary between Cyrenaica and Tripolitania. Axis forces would never pass this way again. Muammar Gaddafi had the arch demolished in the early 1970s. (9 HAA Archive)

Mark Carter in 2007.

work was dangerous. Could you blame us if we sometimes asked ourselves – why are we not doing all this for Wales? Our beautiful valleys were turned into slag heaps. The whole of South Wales, once so green, was drilled, blasted and broken. We used to scrabble about on the rubbish tips looking for scraps of coal to keep ourselves warm, but no amount of coal can keep you warm when your belly's empty. One day the Prince of Wales came to see us and fine words were spoken but nothing was done to alleviate our terrible standard of living. Sometimes I wondered whether the 'Prince of Wales' was not just a pretty title set up to con the Welsh people into falling into line with their English masters!'

'So you've hacked out a sack or two of coal!,' McAlister sneered. 'How would you like to chip the ice off a ship at five in the morning before you could even start a day's work?'

A cold voice on the tannoy brought us back to earth. 'Take cover, Stukas!'

A scream as the leading plane dived. Hundreds of vehicles were scattered all over the place and men ran for cover but there was no cover. Nobody wanted to shelter beneath their trucks because they were scared of the petrol tank. The bombs tumbled out and the desert erupted into sheets of flame. There was no ack ack. The anti-aircraft guns had been used against Rommel's tanks and now these guns were strewn across the desert, broken, rusting pieces of ordnance which also marked the final resting places of their crews.

A hail of machine-gun and small-arms fire followed the planes. We had recently captured a heavy Italian machine gun and we wanted to try it out. Corbett and McAlister struggled with the gigantic belt of cartridges. They got the thing to fire but the recoil almost knocked them off the lorry. The big tracer bullets tore into the sky like meteorites.

Everybody blazed off at those planes and the ordinary rifle fire must have been almost as effective as a machine gun. Black smoke poured out of one of the aircraft and the pilot tried to bring it down. He just missed a couple of lorries before making a crash landing in the desert. He climbed down and ran for it and the plane exploded and blew him off his feet but I think he was O.K.

When the planes had gone we found a shallow wadi and got our remaining guns ready for action. Tubby Wilson asked me to go forward with him to reconnoitre the area with a view to setting up an OP. We were driving slowly to avoid raising too much dust when an eight-wheeled German armoured car came out of a dip in the ground about 300 yards in front of us. An eight-wheeler is a fast heavily-armed vehicle and I knew we wouldn't stand a chance if we tried to run for it. The armoured car halted while the crew tried to decide whether we were friend or foe. We were a pretty bedraggled looking lot without tin hats and as luck would have it the sun was behind us. Maybe they thought we were their own troops bringing in a captured British vehicle. Then, glancing into the mirror, I noticed with a jolt that another eight-wheeler had lurched into view some 200 yards behind us. 'Wave!' Wilson hissed at me.

I lit a cigarette, puffed out clouds of smoke, and gave them a friendly wave. We drove on slowly, half expecting a shell to blow us sky high but we were lucky once again. After a mile or two we came across more German vehicles and Wilson decided that it was impossible to set up an OP anywhere here, so we turned round and drove back. Meanwhile an Australian infantry battalion with a brigade of tanks had been moving up behind us and we had to thread our way through their transport. Apparently the Germans were about to launch another big attack and this time the Aussies had been called in to repel it. We halted for a while so as not to get in the way of all that stuff they were bringing up and as a result we were able to watch their tanks go forward. Suddenly the desert in front of us became full of men as the Australian infantry followed behind the tanks. There were hundreds of them, the sun catching their bayonets. Whistles blew as they came on, waving their rifles wildly and yelling at the tops of their voices – like the crowd at a football match when a goal has been scored.

The German machine guns opened up then and big gaps appeared in the lines of charging men. The Australians met the enemy infantry in a savage hand-to-hand battle, lunging and stabbing with their bayonets and swinging their rifle butts. I saw one man light a petrol-soaked rag on his homemade incendiary bomb and throw it on top of a tank. A tinkle of broken glass and the burning liquid ran down one of the ventilator shafts. There was a heavy thud and a flame shot out of the tank like a plumber's blow lamp. Then came a much bigger explosion. The hatch was flung open and the crew of four scrambled out, their clothing on fire, and rolled about on the ground. That tank quickly became an inferno and everybody hurried to get clear before the ammunition went up.

Then developed a mighty slogging match of tank against tank until the desert was littered with blazing hulks and the infantry, without the tanks to shelter behind, became more exposed to machine-gun fire. A great cloud of dust and smoke hung like a pall over what was already an open graveyard. Wilson decided that our only chance of linking up with the rest of the army was to bring our guns up and follow the Australian attack through under cover of darkness. In other words it would be better to tag along with the Australians than to hang about in a kind of no man's land with the enemy forces all round us.

Our guns were still there in their well-camouflaged positions in the wadi and we hooked them up and prepared to move out. Wilson and I drove on ahead, the guns followed. The still burning tanks provided us with all the light we needed. Dead and wounded littered the desert. We picked up what men we could and left water with those who were dying. When I looked up at the stars their cold glitter seemed to mock me. They had seen it all before and their message hung like a banner across the sky: mankind, the main enemy, had been doomed from the start.

Once during the night we drew up alongside some British lorries. The crews were stretched out asleep close by. We were about to jump down when Wilson noticed the coal-scuttle helmets lying about. We managed to reverse out of there without raising the alarm and we brought our guns round in a wide detour clear of the camp. Later we passed another line of German vehicles but it was very dark and nobody challenged us. They must have thought we were their own men bringing in some captured British guns.

The day dawned with black smoke blotting out the sky and we found ourselves caught up in a vast movement of disorganized and fleeing troops to the east. Trucks, lorries, tanks and motorcyclists were all mixed up together and the rumours were rife: Rommel had broken through and was thrusting deep into Egypt and the entire Eighth Army had been cut off. A survivor from 4 Armoured Brigade told us how his brigade together with all its tanks had been captured the night before.

The brigade had been moving back through the darkness and because it was difficult to see where they were going in the rough stony desert they halted to wait for daylight. It was then that tanks from an advancing Panzer regiment came up to within about thirty yards of the British armour. At first both sides thought the other friendly. The Germans then realized that they had run into a big concentration of British tanks and acted swiftly. Their tanks surrounded the exhausted and confused British and turned on their searchlights. Armoured cars then raced in among the vehicles. Men jumped down with grenades and automatic weapons and under the glare of the searchlights began to take prisoners. There were some bursts of fire and one or two tanks tried to drive off but were quickly shot up and destroyed. This capture in the middle of the night of an entire British armoured brigade was one of the little known disasters of the desert war and was, of course, played down at the time.

Tanks can't run without petrol and the German push ground to a halt. The war in Russia had been given priority over everything and their troops in North Africa had to go short of petrol and other essential supplies. The British commanding general managed to put the broken pieces of the Eighth Army together and somewhere south-east of Halfaya Pass we consolidated and made a stand. Two weeks later, when the line had stabilized, we pulled back for a short distance for refitting and maintenance work.

Sergeant Major Palmer came up to me. 'Take a couple of your men and go down to Sidi Barrani. You're to pick up a new gun for yourself. Your old gun will go to Number Two crew to replace the one that was lost. Put Buckley in charge here. I'll see that you get a movement order. You should be able to pick that gun up and be back here within a few days!'

I stared at that wilderness of sand. I found it difficult to breathe. Sidi Barrani. A hospital. An Australian girl with the radiance of the Sea of Tasman on her brow…Mary-Anne. I had more or less written her off.

I pulled out that old handkerchief. The perfume she'd put there still lingered. Well, if I was really going to Sidi Barrani maybe I should call at the hospital and see her. I told Rule to come with me. Although he had been on leave fairly recently he looked pale and washed out and a short break in Sidi Barrani might do him good.

And I chose McAlister to come along too because he would be a good standby in the event of a breakdown.

We started early the next day but the journey took much longer than expected. We discovered that we couldn't use the coast road because at that time all traffic coming up to the front had priority. The highway now was a one-way road and everything travelling eastward was counted as non-productive. We had, therefore, to find our way to Sidi Barrani across the desert.

We had started out with almost a full tank of petrol which should have been ample. However, low-gear work across the rough boulder-strewn desert had drunk most of that up. Eventually we found a petrol dump close to the main road. A long column of vehicles was waiting to be tanked up. At the entrance of the office a crowd of officers and NCOs stood about brandishing papers and demanding petrol. The sergeant in charge was desperately trying to keep cool. His orders, direct from Army Headquarters, were not to supply petrol to any transport other than armoured fighting vehicles, staff cars and ambulances and then only providing they were travelling westwards towards the front.

A bunch of red-faced swearing majors, colonels and brigadiers stood there shouting that they had urgent business and must not be delayed a moment longer. They fingered the holsters of their revolvers, all of them itching to shoot down this cheeky sergeant and grab the petrol for themselves. What chance had I, a mere NCO travelling eastward in a 15-hundredweight truck? I took my place in the queue but everytime I got a little closer to the petrol sergeant one of the officers elbowed me out of the way. In the end I started to get worked up too.

'I've got to pick up a gun in Sidi Barrani and bring it up to the bloody front!' I shouted. Nobody seemed to take any notice and I doubt very much whether anybody believed me.

Meanwhile Rule and McAlister had not been idle. Bombed and shelled vehicles seemed to litter the desert and not far up the road they found a wrecked lorry which still had some petrol in its tank. We drew up alongside and managed to siphon off enough to see us to Sidi Barrani.

I was torn between going along to see Mary-Anne at the hospital or reporting to the ordnance depot. If I signed for the new gun I would be expected to take delivery of it straight away. I certainly couldn't risk parking it at the hospital while I went in to see Mary-Anne. A 25-pounder field gun parked up there would bring the Red Caps swarming like bees round a jam jar. I decided to see Mary-Anne first and, after dropping Rule and McAlister off at the NAAFI, I drove on up to the hospital. Mary-Anne had moved on. I learned that she had volunteered to work in Tobruk and had travelled there a few weeks previously. Tobruk – that besieged fortress which had survived a holocaust of bombing and shelling. I don't suppose I'd see Mary-Anne again. She'd volunteered for the worst place on earth.

When I called at the ordnance depot they told me that the convoy which had brought the gun to Egypt had been late. The 25-pounder would be in Sidi Barrani in about five days' time. The officer in charge said he would send a message back to my unit to enquire whether I should wait there in Sidi Barrani or return to my unit. Back came the message that I should wait. They were probably concerned that, if I didn't stay there and collect the gun, some other unit would grab it. Five days in Sidi Barrani. There was nothing to do. The sea was too cold for swimming and there was not even a mobile cinema.

I toyed with the idea of hitch-hiking to Alexandria. Trouble was I had no pass and very little money. Worse, if the Red Caps caught me I would be charged with desertion. And as for Mary-Anne – now that she wasn't there I discovered that I wanted to see her more than ever. I decided to go along to the NAAFI and get drunk.

McAlister was there drinking whisky. Rule put down a large John Collins and looked at me guiltily. I bought a bottle of whisky, took it across to the table and banged it down. McAlister looked up at me with a new interest.

'Something bothering you, Sarge?'

I told him about Mary-Anne and how I expected to find her in Sidi Barrani and that she had gone to work at a hospital in Tobruk.

'And to make things, worse the blasted gun hasn't even left Alex yet. It'll take at least five days before they sort it all out and get it up here!'

'So what are we supposed to do, hang about in this dump?' McAlister grumbled.

'That's right. I had a message from the regiment. We're to wait here and pick it up.'

'Let's hitch a lift to Alex and have some fun. We can be there by morning.'

'No pass,' I reminded him.

'What the hell. It's not our fault we're stuck here. If we're stopped we can prove we had to wait about for that gun.'

'We'd be hundreds of miles behind the line. You know what the bloody Red Caps are like. Without papers we'd all be in the can – on a charge of desertion!'

McAlister took another swig and a cunning look came into his eyes. 'You wanted to see that girlfriend of yours eh? Well, you've got five days. Why don't you slip over to Tobruk and surprise her? You can be in and out of there in five days easy.'

I could tell that McAlister wanted to get rid of me. He wasn't scared of going to Alex!

'Don't be daft, the Germans have got it all bottled up.'

'I meant you could get there by sea. I was talking to those two Aussies at the bar. They've just got in from Tobruk for a spot of leave and they told me there were boats going in and out of there all the time.'

Rule and McAlister got up to follow me as I made my way across to the bar. The Australians, one short, one tall, their uniforms torn and filthy, their faces unshaved, looked as if they'd just climbed out of a bomb-gutted building. They stared unsmilingly at me and didn't want to know about Tobruk. I bought them both a drink and asked them if it was possible to go there by boat.

'The boats go day and night,' the tall one who was called Ed, informed me. 'Most of them get sunk!'

I gulped down my drink and poured myself another. Maybe I'd be lucky. Maybe I could spend those five days in Tobruk! And if anything went wrong, if I were arrested, well, being in a front-line fortress like Tobruk would hardly be the same as being caught way behind the lines in a place like Alex. I told the two Aussies about Mary-Anne and how I was stuck here in Sidi Barrani for five days because I had to wait and pick up a gun.

'When's the best time to go?' I asked them.

The two men exchanged glances and shook their heads. If I hadn't mentioned Mary-Anne I think they would have told me to go to hell!

'He's crazy,' the small one who was called Bud exclaimed. 'Still if he wants to see his girl...'

'The best time to go is tonight,' Ed said. 'There's a destroyer loading up now and they're taking back a bunch of cobbers who have been on leave together with some replacements.

'You'll need a pass to get in there – especially if you want to get out!' Bud said.

I cursed. 'I hadn't thought of that!'

The two Aussies put their heads together and muttered something and then Ed swung round on me. 'Why don't you borrow mine, cobber? I'm here for seven days so when you get back from seeing your girl friend you can give it back to me.'

This was typical of the Australians. They sometimes had a casual way of putting things but they were among the most genuine men that I had ever met. It was McAlister who settled it for me.

'What have you got to lose? Sooner or later the Germans are going to take that place and if they do you'll never see her again.'

It was tempting. Although Rule and McAlister said they would stay in Sidi Barrani and keep in touch with the Ordnance Depot, I knew that McAlister, at any rate, would be off on the spree. But I was still worried. The Aussie was taking a big risk and I would feel better about it if I could repay him in some way.

'What can I do for you then?'

The Australian took a long pull at his cigarette. 'You can buy us the next round mate!'

Before I left Ed lent me his bush hat too. It is surprising what that rakish colonial style headgear can do for you and when I caught my reflection in the bar mirror I looked like an Australian too.

I said goodbye to Rule and McAlister and warned them that if they did leave Sidi Barrani they would be on their own, but if anything went wrong and they were caught, I would do everything I could to get them out of trouble and safely back to the battery providing they told nobody about my trip to Tobruk, and we shook hands on it and parted company.

Late that evening I joined the queue of men and we filed up the gangway and went on board the destroyer. We had to show our passes.

'But you've only just arrived!' the boarding sergeant exclaimed as he examined my pass. 'What, fed up with your leave already?'

'Left my wallet behind mate. You can't buy any tucker without yer swag and the Birka don't exactly put it on the slate neither''

The sergeant nodded sympathetically. 'That's tough. Never mind, with a little luck you could be back here again tomorrow or the next day!'

The destroyer was crammed with reinforcements and leave men returning from a short break and we waited there while she got up steam for the quick dash to Tobruk. The ship's guns were manned and everybody was ordered to wear lifejackets. I was told that we stood less than a fifty-fifty chance of getting through the bombing and the minefields, let alone the shelling from enemy shore batteries.

I stood by the rail and stared at the black tossing water. All this in order to see a girl who had probably forgotten me by now. I remembered that I had to be back within five days. Maybe I should change my mind and get off that boat while I still had the chance. Next minute they were pulling up the gangway and, somehow, I felt an odd sense of relief.

In addition to the troops who crowded the destroyer's decks, a number of armoured cars and even tanks had been hoisted on board and made fast. A huge amount of shells of various calibre had also been taken on board as well as hundreds of tins of petrol. And there were crates of food and NAAFI supplies and boxes of Red Cross hospital equipment – almost every kind of commodity essential for a beleaguered garrison. The ship was, in fact, heavily overloaded and when we left the shelter of the harbour the seas came right over her decks. We clung on to whatever we could find and were soaked.

Because of her huge cargo the destroyer could only make about 15 knots and after three or four hours of pitching and rolling we could see a reddish glow in the western sky. Tobruk! The most bombed and shelled town on earth. A town which, with a handful of UK and Commonwealth troops, had held out against the might of the Axis army for almost a year.

As we drew close the ship became bathed in the light from blazing buildings and warehouses and it was not long before the first Stukas came screaming out of the sky. Their bombs straddled the ship and she rolled drunkenly.

We all felt pretty helpless. There were no slit trenches to dive into and nowhere you could go; and just then the desert, for all its terror, seemed a better place to be. The bombs fell so close that we were deluged with sea water. The ship was already top-heavy and a direct hit would probably have been enough to send her to the bottom.

The Stukas came round again, machine guns blazing, and we dived behind the vehicles that were lashed there as the bullets ripped a trail across the decks, smashing into the bridge superstructure, severing cables and making us all duck. I remembered all those petrol tins which were stacked up forward and the tons of field artillery ammunition and I knew that it would take only one of those bullets to blow us all sky high. However, the shore defences were sending up such a barrage of steel that the planes finally unloaded what was left of their bombs on the town and flew off.

Next we had to run the gauntlet of the German shore batteries and everybody was ordered below decks as the first shells burst around the ship. Down there we were packed like sardines and if the ship had gone down we wouldn't have stood a chance. The destroyer answered the fire with her guns and once she was hit below the waterline but she continued to make headway and soon began to nose her way past the wrecked and partly-submerged ships which cluttered up the harbour.

It was like coming into Dante's Inferno. The guns on the perimeter were firing non-stop, the explosions echoing and re-echoing across the harbour while the flames from the burning town bathed the destroyer in an eerie light. A line was thrown ashore and we filed up on deck. The stink of cordite and the burnt and blasted metalwork hung about the ship and made us choke. The dockside was crowded with workers and already a crane was alongside the ship.

The Military Police at the bottom of the gangway barely glanced at my borrowed pass. Maybe this was because I was heading in the right direction and I wondered if things would be so easy when my time came to depart. I was told to join some men who were waiting to board a truck. They were Australians, all from the same regiment, men who had returned from a short break from the fighting. We climbed into the back of the truck. Most of the men were pretty tight and the fact that I was a stranger didn't seem to bother anybody and, after all, I could have been a replacement. Then an officer climbed in beside the driver and he turned round to face us.

'Sorry you lot but you've got to go straight back into the line. The bastards have been putting in a big attack and some of their tanks almost broke through the perimeter yesterday. Looks like we're set to kick 'em to hell and breakfast tomorrow morning!'

My heart gave a lurch and I felt weak all over. I began to wonder what on earth I had let myself in for. I had been pitchforked into the poor bloody infantry and it had all been my own doing. It looked as if I had really landed myself up the creek this time. If I tried to tell anybody that I came over here to see my girlfriend and that I had to get back to collect a 25-pounder field gun they would have brought in the white coated men.

The truck threaded its way through the bombed and shell-shattered streets where the smoke hung like a fog and hardly a building was left standing. The crash of artillery and the rattle of machine guns echoed across the town like some monstrous firework display. The last stage of the journey to the perimeter was made on foot. The thirty-five mile perimeter defences consisted of a huge network of trenches, barbed-wire entanglements, minefields and gun positions. Many of these defences were on the escarpment which overlooked the town while on the flat ground below the hulks of burnt-out tanks had been converted into command posts and machine-gun nests. We were informed that a recent attack had been repulsed in hand-to-hand fighting and that all available troops in the Tobruk garrison had been put into the perimeter to replace the heavy losses.

For me all this was like a bad dream. Instead of what seemed to be a fairly safe bet – a quick dash to see Mary-Anne on my borrowed papers and then back on the next leave boat, I suddenly found myself going into the Tobruk perimeter with the Australian infantry. Here I was a complete stranger and so far nobody had questioned my credentials. I suppose it was like that situation whereby traffic was allowed priority providing it was travelling towards the front line. Anything going in the opposite direction was dirt.

The Australians were a good crowd to get on with and, like ourselves, they were pretty easy-going in the front line. You could take your shirt off, smoke and do anything you liked. They had a reputation for being a wild bunch, however, and the Germans feared them, especially when they came at them with bayonets.

We were negotiating a shallow trench close to the forward positions when I realized that I was the only man without a weapon. However, it was getting dark and I managed to pick up a rifle and some spare magazines when nobody was looking. At dawn tomorrow we were going to attack. The countdown was on and I had just four days to get back to Sidi Barrani.

But the Germans, as thorough as ever and determined to succeed this time, beat us to it and just before dawn hundreds of guns started to blast our positions. Our forward positions were mere holes in the ground and here we were pinned down under a hail of screaming, hissing, whirring shrapnel. Stones, boulders and complete sections of barbed-wire entanglements together with their supporting posts were blown into the air. Men, vehicles and guns were pulverized under a hurricane of exploding metal.

The sun came up and the bombardment went on. Many of the holes were only big enough for one or two men and our joints ached and we became stiff with cramp as we huddled there. The red-hot chunks of metal hummed and whizzed about us and we forgot everything. We forgot our families, forgot our girlfriends and we even forgot who we were because the only thing that mattered was how to squeeze another inch or two out of our shallow ditches, and only those who could somehow get below ground level stood any chance of survival.

When the barrage lifted and began to search out our rear defences the mortars started to bombard us. We could see the bombs arcing high overhead like flying fish, the sun catching their fins, and the ground shook under the avalanche of high explosive. The man next to me was trembling, his face ashen, and his hands were shaking so much that he could hardly hold his rifle. I found myself clinging on to my rifle as if it was all between me and a thousand-foot drop. We both knew that, sooner or later, if we didn't get out of there one of those bombs would drop into our hole and blow us into eternity.

We were pinned to the ground and almost driven out of our minds by the din when there was a pause in the mortar fire and, except for the banging of field guns, I could hear only the cries and curses of the wounded. My companion lit a cigarette and I brought out my pipe and got that going.

The whine of engines, the clatter of tank tracks, the stink of hot oil.

'Tanks!'

The cry was carried from one hole to the other. It was heard in Battalion Headquarters and from there it was passed back to the waiting guns.

'Tanks!'

The alarm spread like lightning into the rear areas and then into the town itself and the population reacted as if a bush fire was about to engulf them. I saw one of the iron-clad monsters bulldoze its way through a whole mass of barbed wire and then, with the wire draped all over it, disappear into the murk behind us. Another tank loomed up through the smoke and one of the Australian officers climbed out of his trench and blew his whistle.

'Out! Out! Get out! Don't waste ammunition on the tanks. Let them go past you. Our guns will handle them. Watch out for the infantry!'

That was his last order. The oncoming tank's machine-gun bullets practically cut him in half.

I scrambled out of the hole but the man behind me yelled out that his foot had gone to sleep and I had to stop and pull him out. The tanks rumbled on. Men flung themselves out of the way and one or two of the wilder types climbed up on top and if they couldn't get the hatch open they pushed their grenade into the muzzle of the gun and then jumped off. Other men, caught out in the open, leapt back into their holes only to be crushed into pulp when one of the steel monsters swivelled round on top of them.

Then the tanks were past us and the guns behind us started to take them on over open sights. These gun crews, too, had been taken by surprise and in their frantic haste to engage the enemy had raised the elevation of their barrels too high. The result was that we received more than one salvo of shells from our own side which killed and wounded several men. We lay flat on the ground listening to the fierce battle behind us, hardly daring to breathe. We were so strung up and jittery that we had forgotten to spit out our cigarettes and I knew that I had practically bitten through the stem of my pipe.

They started shelling us again then and I flung myself down behind a ledge of rock. It was all I could find but for me it was like

Everest. After about fifteen minutes the shelling lifted. The whistle blew again and we stood ready to meet another attack. I tried to lift my rifle but my left arm felt as if a knitting needle had been thrust into it and I noticed that the blood was running off the end of my sleeve like a tap. That, and the early morning exertion on an empty stomach, was probably why I acted like a drunk and it was then that I discovered that I couldn't stand up on my own two feet.

CHAPTER SEVEN

The hospital, in spite of its Red Cross signs and drapes, was a bombed and shell-shattered building open mostly to the sky. Here, under a tarpaulin roof, in what had once been the kitchen, the surgeon and his assistant laboured hour after weary hour. The surgeon chain-smoked because this was the only way he could keep going. Now and again his assistant would reach across and wipe the sweat from his face or put another cigarette into his mouth and light it for him. The atmosphere in the room was thick with tobacco smoke, the smell of anaesthetics and the stench of wounds. Outside, a long queue of wounded awaited their turn and they lay along the pavements and their stretchers filled the town square.

The surgeon was a young man who had recently flown out to North Africa after finishing his training. He worked with scalpel and saw under a single hanging bulb. He cut through ligaments, tied up veins, stitched up wounds, sawed off arms, sawed off legs. He had passed his exams only by the skin of his teeth but the Royal College would have been impressed with what he was doing now. Sometimes, when the bombing started, the bulb would flicker and go out and then he would work by candlelight or paraffin lamp. Buckets of water were used to swill down the table and more buckets were used for carting away the pieces of flesh and sawn-off limbs. One man was brought in with a stomach wound. A hopeless case. A great wad of field dressing was placed over the wound and the surgeon jerked his thumb.

'Next!'

This, too, was a stomach wound. The bullet had gone through the front and out of the back. The man was alive but unconscious. The surgeon swore. He did what he could to clean and plug the wound but the man would die anyway. He was put on a stretcher and taken outside to lie with the other hopeless cases. In due course they would be loaded up on to a lorry and taken to some waste ground where a mechanical digger was working overtime.

The light from the solitary bulb shone on the exhausted face of the surgeon. His assistant removed the soggy butt end of his cigarette and placed another between his lips.

'Next!'

A young soldier was carried in who had had a miraculous escape. The bullet had gone through the back of his head, and missing every vital section of the brain, had come out through his mouth. All he suffered was a serious but clean flesh wound plus a couple of missing front teeth which the bullet had sheared off on its way out. Four weeks later he was downing his beer in the NAAFI canteen.

'Next!'

The next was me. After waiting all day in the queue I stepped inside that butcher's shop. Anybody who could walk was small fry for the surgeon and he paused to drag a little longer on his cigarette. I climbed on to what looked like a sacrificial altar where he proceeded to remove several small slivers of steel from my arm. After bandaging me up he told me to report to the convalescent camp in town. All my dreams of a beautiful nurse – Mary-Anne in fact – looking after me, had come to nothing. Afterwards I had quite a job finding her.

'Mary-Anne, the girl from Tasmania? She's working out there somewhere.'

I went outside. Men were lying about on the pavements. I could only see one light. An army chaplain was shining a small torch as he went about his business. The thin wafers of bread which he had started out with had long since crumpled in his trembling hands but he gave a pinch to those who could swallow.

He also carried with him a bottle of warm sandy wine. He prayed and he listened to what they had to say. All most of them wanted was a cigarette and he carried a few packets of those too.

I smoked my pipe to steady myself up a little as I made my way along that street. Another light. Somebody bending over a stretcher. An Arab going through some poor devil's pockets? No, it was a woman, her face pale and ghostly in the darkness and she wore nurse's uniform. It was Mary-Anne. She shone her torch at me.

'I thought you were an Arab!' She looked startled.

I was dirty and unshaven and my arm was in a sling. At first she didn't recognize me.

'I thought you were an Arab too!' I could smell that same delicious perfume and maybe it was my voice or my brand of tobacco that gave me away because she came up close to me and shone her torch again.

'For goodness sake. What on earth are you doing here in Tobruk?'

I told her about my trip to Sidi Barrani and my visit to the hospital there. When I told her that an Australian lent me his pass and that I had come across by boat and then ended up in a scrap on the perimeter she thought I was crazy.

'But your regiment. You could be arrested as a deserter.'

'Not if I'm back in Sidi Barrani in a couple of days. Besides,' I tapped my bad arm, 'this is proof that I haven't been swanning around in the wrong direction!'

That evening when she came off duty we met in the Australian Club. The place was blacked out and lit by candlelight and for the first time that day I could really see her. She was quiet at first and didn't say much. She looked tired, older somehow, and her smile was a little sadder than before.

Pictures by the Old Masters were often sad, they were beautiful too, and maybe the candles had something to do with it but that evening I thought the same about Mary-Anne.

Most of the men in that club were just out of the line for a few hours and the din was appalling. The piano never seemed to stop. Everybody knew that the Germans were likely to break through in their next big attack and they shouted and sang as if every minute was their last. That place was like the third class bar on the *Titanic* after all the boats had gone.

I counted those minutes too. Tomorrow I would have to get out of Tobruk. Mary-Anne said she would fix up my arm with a new dressing, and, with luck, that should see me through until I reached Sidi Barrani. After that I didn't care what happened. I would take delivery of the new gun and with McAlister and Rule tow it back to our position. There would be questions about my arm of course but the explanation was simple. We had gone off course a little on our way to Sidi Barrani and had run into a spot of enemy shelling.

But I was worried about Mary-Anne and what the Germans would do to her if they did march in. I tried to persuade her to get out, to come with me, because she would be much safer in that hospital in Sidi Barrani. It was no good. Mary-Anne wouldn't leave Tobruk whatever the odds.

For a moment I toyed with the idea of staying on in Tobruk. Then I remembered that I had a gun to collect in Sidi Barrani and McAlister and Rule would be looking out for me. And I had promised the Australian that I would be back in good time to return his pass to him. Besides, if I did stay on and the Germans captured the town I would probably end up as a prisoner of war, Mary-Anne would disappear and I would never see her again. No. I knew I had to go but, somehow, for me, it was the *Titanic* again and leaving Mary-Anne was like jumping into one of those last boats.

'If the Germans broke through they would ship you off to Europe.'

'They wouldn't harm me, a nurse, it would be against the Geneva Convention. Besides I've been looking after their wounded too.'

I suppose I couldn't blame her and I admired her courage for wanting to come here in the first place.

The Australians had cleared a space in the middle of the room and were taking it in turns to dance with the few women who were present. They soon began to get restless, however, and one of the men came over to our table.

'Want to dance? He's no bloody good with only one arm.'

I cursed because I didn't want anybody waltzing Mary-Anne out of my life – not tonight. All I had left were a few precious hours and once the Aussies started in on her I might as well call it a day.

'I was just about to dance with her myself. My other arm's OK.'

'What, dance with only one arm?' He turned and faced the others. 'Hey fellers, we've got a one-armed dancer!' He laughed. 'So your left arm don't know what your right arm doeth? Maybe it's to squeeze her just a little bit tighter, eh?'

I was still feeling jittery after being messed about by that surgeon and I lost my temper and gave him a push which sent him staggering.

'I could show you a thing or two without any arms.' I said His language made me cringe with Mary-Anne sitting there and I could only hope that she didn't know the meaning of those words he used.

Anyway, he'd have made mincemeat out of me if she hadn't stepped in and accepted his invitation to dance.

After that I had to sit and watch the Australians take it in turns to dance with her. I watched my precious evening go down the drain too. All I could hope for now was to take her back to the hospital when the place shut down for the night.

It was an air raid that settled it and I managed to grab her as the sirens went and the room emptied. We didn't bother to look for a shelter because the bombs were dropping some distance away in the harbour area. It was past midnight and she was on duty in a few hours so I took her back to the hospital. She said I could spend the rest of the night in one of the rooms there but after a while I couldn't sleep so I got up and wandered outside. The town was teeming with activity. Tanks, guns and lorries which had just arrived by ship rattled through the streets while searchlights criss-crossed overhead as they probed the night sky. Australian troops rampaged through the town singing and shouting. Men who had come out of the perimeter waited about for lorries to take them to the rest camps while other troops lined the streets waiting for transport to take them to the front. I noticed a long queue down by the docks and wondered what my chances would be when the time came for me to leave. I chatted and drank beer with groups of Australians and I had a hearty breakfast with them in one of their canteens. I shall never forget that night in Tobruk.

Later that day Mary-Anne dressed my arm at the hospital. She tore off a piece of paper and scribbled down the address of an aunt in London.

'I plan to visit her after the war. If we don't meet up again over here you can show me round London.'

She said that she would only be in England for a few weeks because she planned to return to Australia. After that I didn't see much of her because she was too busy – but she did come down to the docks to see me off. I joined the queue for the only ship that was leaving that night, an ex-passenger cargo vessel named the *Valera*. It was rather a sad business that parting because neither of us knew if we would ever see each other again.

With my arm in a sling I was lucky. I showed my borrowed pass – nobody seemed to notice that it was four days' old already – put on an Australian accent and was told to hurry up the gangway. When I arrived on deck I looked back. She stood there slim and very pretty in her nurse's uniform. I shall always remember the smile that was in her eyes and on her lips and somehow that last glimpse of her seemed to make the whole trip worthwhile.

The ship, after feeling her way along the narrow channel between the partly-sunken wrecks, headed out on a course running parallel with the coast. Maybe it is the throb of engines or the sudden splash of wash on the shore but a vigilant enemy, peering into the night, can often make out the dark moving bulk of a ship even if she is blacked out. The German gunners had only to send over some star shells to spotlight our ship – a nice slow moving target – and then they started to range on us. The ship's guns fired back with what weapons they had – an old 4.5 naval gun mounted at the stern and a couple of Bofors.

The *Valera* was an old tub and the most she could make was about 14 knots. We soon came under heavy fire and more coal was shovelled into the furnaces until the boilers were almost bursting. The engines clanged and groaned like some infernal machine. Somebody told me afterwards that the *Valera* had in fact got up to 20 knots on that particular night. Although my life depended on her staying afloat I couldn't help feeling sorry for the boat and I knew that if she was sunk by the Germans at least she would have cheated the knackers' yard and gone to an honourable grave.

We had left Tobruk at 8 p.m. and arrived in Sidi Barrani at 1 a.m. Pretty good going for the *Valera*. After we disembarked I went straight to the NAAFI which I knew would be open all night, and sure enough, the two Australians, Ed and Budd, were sitting at the bar. Ed glanced round and grinned when he saw me. I went across to join them. Ed shot an appreciative look at my arm.

'Been in a scrap mate?'

'I suppose you could call it that, yes.'

I gave him back his pass and hat which he'd lent me and bought them both brandies and cigars. Sidi Barrani is a small place and any news seems to find its way into the NAAFI. I learned that McAlister had hitched a lift to Alex. Rule on the other hand had stayed in Sidi Barrani but got himself into some kind of trouble. Apparently he had been caught out of bounds in one of the local brothels and was being held by the Military Police. I was also informed that the Sergeant from the Ordnance Depot had been looking for me because the new gun had arrived and he wanted me to sign for it and take it away.

All this put a bit of a damper on things but there was nothing I could do about it now. All I wanted was to hit the hay so I made myself comfortable on one of the sofas, wrapped my greatcoat round me and went out like a light. I seemed to sleep for an eternity. I dreamt that I was back on the operating table and the surgeon was trying to take my arm off with a saw. I awoke in agony. The Sergeant from Ordnance was shaking me. When I threw off my greatcoat and he saw my arm he apologized.

'That twenty-five pounder of yours has arrived and if you don't hurry up and take delivery of it some other mob will get it.'

I knew the danger well enough. It would only take some white-kneed young officer just out from England to commandeer it to put me in a right fix. But even if I got help to hook the gun up to my truck I doubt whether I could drive all the way back to my unit with only one hand. I needed Rule and McAlister to help with the heavy work. And even if I could manage on my own how could I return to my unit without an explanation as to their whereabouts? If they discovered that I had been to Tobruk I would be on the carpet with a vengeance.

My truck was still parked where I had left it. I found it difficult to manage with only one hand but eventually I drove it across to the Ordnance Depot and backed it up close to the new gun. Then I went into the office and signed for it.

'Could you give me a hand to hook it up?' I asked the Sergeant in charge, 'my men are just having a last drink in the NAAFI.'

He helped me lift the trail and hook it on to the truck. It didn't seem to bother him that my arm was in a sling. He was only too glad to get the gun off his hands. I drove it out of the compound and parked it in a quiet place where I could think.

Before me lay several hours of rough driving. If anything went wrong, if I had a puncture or got bogged down I would be useless and I cursed Rule and McAlister. Those two men had let me down, when

I needed them badly. It was no good waiting about for McAlister. He was probably still living it up in Alex or even Cairo. Rule was my only hope. Somehow I had to get him out of that mess. I found my way to the Military Police depot on foot and by then I could have throttled him if I had the chance.

'Gunner Rule? Yes, we're holding him here. He is charged with being out of bounds in the brothel district.'

The MP stared at my furious perspiring face. 'Oh, so you've come for him have you Sergeant?' He started to thumb through some papers and I pulled myself together with a jerk. This was unbelievable luck. He obviously thought I'd come with a collection order from my unit.

'That's right, I've come to take this little bastard back.' I snapped.

I must have looked pretty aggressive and the MP a tough, short-haired disciplinarian, seemed to be quite concerned.

'Hold on Sarge, he was only out of bounds!'

'Anybody who doesn't obey the rules in my lot is for the high jump!'

The Corporal was impressed. 'OK sarge. Wait here and I'll go and fetch him.'

Soon I could hear the 'left right, left right' staccato commands and Rule was quick marched into the office. He looked relieved to see me standing there.

'Oh good old Sarge. Thank God you've come to get me out of this!'

I had to play out my little act to the hilt of course, otherwise the Corporal would have tumbled to my game. I was pretty mad anyway and my arm was giving me jip. I was just in the right mood to teach these lousy MPs a thing or two!

'Stand to attention!' I shouted. 'Don't you good old Sarge me! So you had the neck to go gallivanting around the brothels without permission. You horrible little Welshman. Just wait until I get you into the regimental cooler!'

'May I see your papers?' The Corporal asked me.

I tapped my wounded arm and winced. 'We got shelled on the way over here and we had to run for it. I got some splinters in my arm. The papers were lost but I'll see that you get a duplicate set when I get back. Now, we've got a long drive ahead of us so could you hand over this little creep?'

The Corporal hesitated. Then he nodded. 'Glad to get rid of him.

Now we can get on with handling some real crime around here.'

He pushed some papers over to me. 'Here you are Sarge, sign here.' I signed, handed him back his pen and quick marched Rule out of there.

When we were out of sight of the depot I walked on ahead and he caught up with me.

'I couldn't help it Sarge. After that time in the Birka I couldn't get women out of my mind!'

'The brothels in this dump are worse than the Birka,' I told him. 'The women here must be riddled with it. Why you could pick up a dose just by looking at 'em!'

I had always been careful about swearing at Rule because I had thought he was one of those religious types. I discovered that it was a relief to let go and I said some things that would make even our Geordie cringe. '…and bloody well report to the MO when you get back. That's an order!'

We had a long drive ahead of us so I decided to go into the NAAFI for a drink. Rule tagged along behind me like an obedient dog. One of the first men I saw at the bar there was McAlister knocking back some whisky and I tried to hide my relief.

'What kept you Sarge?' He nodded at my arm. 'What does the other fellow look like?'

He had in fact hitched a lift to Alex and he described how he had spent most of his time in the 'red light' district of Sister Street.

I was tired and depressed and I couldn't be bothered to tell him off. I knocked down a couple of large whiskies and jerked my thumb at the door.

'When you've quite finished…'

We arrived back to find that the Battery had completed their refit and were ready to move forward. The enemy had been falling back steadily while fighting rearguard actions and December ended with the great news that Tobruk had been relieved. I breathed a sigh of relief. Mary-Anne – she was safe!

The Axis retreat continued and when Benghazi fell everybody thought that the Panzerarmee was finished. But Rommel made a stand on the El Brega line where they had launched their first attack against the British nine months ago. Meanwhile, the German garrison at Halfaya Pass had surrendered. The road was now open all the way through from Cairo to Benghazi.

In January the Germans circulated rumours through their agents in Cairo and Alexandria that they were retreating still farther westward. They blew up a few old Italian dumps, set fire to ships in El Brega harbour and sent columns of vehicles back along the road to Tripoli to illustrate the point. It was all a big bluff. Rommel knew that, somehow, he must attack before the British steamrollered them out of North Africa for good. This would be his only chance – a last-ditch gamble.

However, the British lines of communication at this time stretched back for hundreds of miles into Egypt and this presented us with a big problem. The farther westward we advanced the more difficult it became to bring up supplies of petrol and equipment whereas the enemy who had fallen back were now much closer to their main supply base at Tripoli.

Rommel attacked on 21 January. He threw in everything he had got and recaptured Benghazi and, advancing eastward, captured most of the positions they had lost. But again he could not take Tobruk. We stopped him eventually. Both sides were exhausted and the front line settled down to a stalemate at Gazala.

In the desert wounds are slow to heal. I had long since dispensed with my sling for it only invited questions, but my arm was still giving me trouble. As luck would have it we had moved up fairly close to Tobruk and since a road was now open into the town the MO suggested I call at the hospital to have the wound properly dressed.

I had heard that many people, women especially, had been evacuated during the recent scare but I knew that Mary-Anne would be one of the last to leave. I drove into the town and parked the truck. A cold hard rain soaked me as I made my way up to the hospital and I found some shelter in the front porch. I was lucky. One of the attendants, an Italian prisoner of war, told me that she had just come off duty and he went off to fetch her. Like most of us I hadn't had a chance to shave or clean up and at first she didn't recognize me, believing that I was just another casualty. It was the calm face and the peace in those hazel eyes which held me.

'You've heard about the bad penny,' I said.

She stared at me and then she looked up at the rain and smiled.

'Pennies from heaven. I don't see any bad ones!'

CHAPTER EIGHT

The front line continued to be quiet and I was able to slip into Tobruk at least once a week to have my arm dressed. I tried to time this when I knew that Mary-Anne would be off duty and we discovered a quiet little cove below the cliffs where we could picnic and spend a few hours together. Once I got her talking about Australia.

'I believe I told you that my father's big interest was prospecting and he used to go off looking for gold and precious stones. He would thrill me with stories of the untold wealth that is lying about in the outback waiting to be picked up. He once told me that there was an arid stretch of desert in the middle of Australia where gem stones can be picked up by the bucketful.'

She explained that this magic place was about 400 miles north-west of Broken Hill, where the waters of the Georgina and Diamantina meet and go on to flow into Lake Eyre. Almost every kind of gem stone could be found in the beds of the lonely creeks and old water channels which meander through this wasteland for miles before leading into these rivers. Many of the gem stones were only a few inches below the surface. The deeper deposits would be of an even finer quality. Rainwater streaming through these creeks could reveal a veritable hoard of treasure.

'There are one or two snags of course. These gems lie close to an old Aborigine burial ground, and then again a lot of water is needed to wash through the gullies before the gems can be found in any worthwhile quantity, and up there is one of the driest parts of Australia. It hardly ever rains! All the same I plan to go up there after the war and have a look round.'

'What about the blacks?'

'The Aborigines? A white woman would be perfectly safe.'

'Not if you go poking around in their burial places!'

'I shall have to take a chance on that.'

'What sort of gems are they?'

'Opal, sapphire, topaz, zircon, that sort of thing. Maybe just plain diamonds!'

'Did you ever see any of those gems?'

'Oh yes. My father once tipped out a sackful. Some were the size of peas, others as large as marbles. Every colour and combination of colours was there. Many were of an intense blue while some were just a watery white. Others were a deep yellow and a great many had a port-wine tinge. Here and there were some green stones and one or two had a pale straw colour. Sometimes when you picked up a stone you would find that it was translucent with a deep crimson inside. Turn it over and you would see waves of blue green and yellow light.'

My treasure-hunting instincts were aroused and I could already see myself going to Australia after the war. Maybe she'd let me go with her.

'It's pretty wild in the middle of Australia. Your father must have had a rough time crossing those deserts!'

She nodded. 'They call it the Great Thirst Lands. My father once crossed the Sturt desert. His water ran out and the heat was terrible and he nearly died. He was saved by a tree called Ilburra. The Aborigines once told him to look out for it. Apparently if you dig up the roots you can squeeze out some wonderful clear water. In a thirsty land like Australia the Ilburra tree is a tree of life!

Once my father sorted out some dull whitish looking stones from his sack. He thought they were pretty worthless so he threw them on to the rockery. One day an old geologist friend of his turned up for tea. It was hot and they sat outside. The geologist picked up one of those stones and had a good look at it. He told my father that all that stone needed was to be cut and polished because it was a particularly fine diamond. My father was able to retire after that!'

She was silent for a long time. 'My mother died just before the war, my father three months later. I guess he couldn't live without her...'

Mary-Anne had never been to England and I tried to fill her in on some of the beauty spots. I ended up with one of my favourite haunts.

'The north Devon cliffs for instance are among the highest in Britain. There are wild headlands with huge expanses of gorseland and rock. Sometimes the land disappears into deep ravines and all you can hear is the thunder of the Atlantic. Up there, there is nothing between you and the other side of the world!'

She sat there on the sand, hands clasped about her knees, and when I looked into her eyes I knew that it was now or never and I asked her that same old time-battered question. She was nice about it but she brought me down to earth with a jolt.

'You've forgotten. There's a war on. Just look at the map. The way things are going now you and I will probably end up in South Africa!'

This was possible of course. The Germans had occupied almost the whole of Europe and now their armies were pushing through Russia towards the Caucasus. In North Africa Rommel was driving for Egypt and the Persian oilfields. Any chance of getting back to England in the foreseeable future looked pretty bleak.

It was a sad end to a beautiful day but I knew she was right. I was, after all, in a combat unit and she wouldn't want to be married one day and widowed the next! Well, I still had the address she had given me and I told her that one day when the war ended I would look her up when she came to London. I cursed the war and I cursed my luck, too, as I drove out of Trobuk. Was it all going to end like those ships that pass in the night?

I didn't get another chance to visit Tobruk because my battery was ordered south into the Bir Hacheim area. I wrote to Mary-Anne but I never received a reply and as I was probably the only person in the Eighth Army who was posting private letters to Tobruk I began to wonder whether they ever reached her. Meanwhile, both armies were preparing for a big attack and the question kept bothering me. This time, would the Germans take Tobruk?

Bir Hacheim, held by a Brigade of Free French, was the southernmost point of the Gazala Line. This whole line consisted of a number of strongpoints called 'boxes'. Each of these boxes was about a mile square, mined, strewn with barbed-wire entanglements and defended by tanks, guns and infantry. These isolated forts could meet an attack from any direction and if the Germans attacked they would first have to destroy these boxes or risk being caught in their rear by the defenders.

Our gun position at Bir Hacheim was in one of those boxes and our main job down there would be to support some of the new General Grant tanks which were already on their way to us. Until now our tanks had consisted of Valentines, Crusaders and American-built Honeys. The General Grants had a 75mm gun in addition to a 37mm. At last we had something which could really sort out the German Mark III and Mark IV tanks.

I had as good a gun team as any in the desert. Corbett, Buckey and McAlister would go through hell and high water together. Doug Walton, the gravedigger, was a good man too because he was a calm, calculating type and a good gun-layer. Rule had changed. He no longer talked about religion. Over the past few months he had become a tough cynical little Welshman who enjoyed a drink and swore as well as any of us. What concerned me though, as Number One, was the way he threw himself into his job. Maybe he wanted to try and work off some of that sin. He didn't seem all that scared either when the shells were dropping close. Then, again, maybe he still clung to his previous conviction of an afterlife.

The weather began to warm up a little and spring flowers suddenly appeared in the stony desert. From the west came the never-ending sounds of the German build-up; the roar of transport, the clatter of tank tracks, and, at dawn from farther off still, the blast of aircraft engines warming up.

Meanwhile, we were becoming hemmed in by the new units which had been sent up from Cairo. There were more tanks, more guns of every calibre and more motorized infantry until our particular stretch of desert began to resemble a gigantic car park. Men came strolling across to our gun position wanting to borrow tea, milk or sugar or trying to cadge some of our precious water. McAlister took exception to all this and so did most of us. Old campaigners, we guarded our privacy and what little luxuries we had, jealously, and we had no desire to mix it with a crowd of white-kneed rookies just out from England. McAlister told them to keep their distance and they told him where to get off and this led to heated slanging matches and rude two-fingered gestures. Once I had to step in to prevent an all-out fight.

'Listen, we've got enough on our hands with the bloody Germans breathing down our necks. You keep away from us and we'll keep away from you...!'

I also noticed that the two-fingered gestures were getting out of hand and that people were insulting each other at the least possible excuse. I called the warring factions together and told them to keep the peace.

I explained that the palm inwards V sign – not to be confused with Churchill's palm outward V sign – came out of ancient history. When the Normans captured an English archer they cut off the first two fingers of his right hand so that he could never fire an arrow again. After that, whenever an English archer scored a hit he displayed the sign to show that he still had those two fingers.

'So if we capture a German,' somebody put in, 'and cut off all four of his fingers he won't be able to fire anything.'

I agreed. 'And if he were lucky enough to keep those fingers he would probably give you the four-finger sign which of course is not so insulting is it?'

All this helped to calm things down a little, but, as I noticed soon afterwards, far from curing anybody of the deplorable habit it only seemed to make things worse, and the practice became almost a phobia with men exchanging those rude V signs with almost everybody they met. Anyway, I have always thought the palm outward V sign a rather ridiculous and pathetic gesture and I can never understand why it was adopted as a sign of victory in the first place.

By the middle of May both the British and Axis armies were pretty well matched with about 140,000 men and 500 tanks to each side. When the engineers went forward to remove the enemy mines in front of us we knew that time was running out and we would soon be making our big push forward. Those engineers were among the bravest of men. They had to pit their wits against all the wiles of clever German inventiveness and their lives often hung on the tiniest of pressures or the minutest of threads. For these men every turn of the screwdriver was a step across eternity. One had to reckon that every single mine was booby trapped in some way or another and there were many subtle and deadly ways of fooling our engineers. One of the most common was to plant one mine on top of another so that when the first mine was lifted the other went up.

Food was always a problem. The ration truck was often missing and then we had to scrounge and scrape the best we could. Sometimes we bought eggs and bread from the wandering Bedouin who, incidentally, thought we were crazy to fight the Germans over what seemed to them to be just a useless stretch of waterless desert. When we were hungry one of the quickest ways of preparing a meal was to get hold of some flour and water, mix it into a dough and then put the mixture into the hot embers of our fire and leave to bake.

We added this and that, whatever we had, to this 'bread' and it was always hot and delicious.

The May heat together with the food and general living conditions for thousands of men brought an even worse plague of flies. It was no good trying to brush them away. They swarmed everywhere and they could give you a painful nip. It was always very difficult to eat or drink and I knew that many of us would sooner face the enemy than be eaten alive by those 'Gypo' pests. It soon became so hot that the tank crews could fry their eggs on the steel plating of their tanks. The water in our water bottles was hot too and the only way to get a decent drink was to have a brew up.

We had just got a nice brew up going when I noticed a big cloud of dust on the horizon. Another blasted sandstorm and it was coming this way. As if the flies and the heat were not enough! I could almost feel that gritty stuff on my teeth already. The tank crews had seen it too and they quickly scooped up their eggs and hurried to cover up the rest of their food.

The dust cloud, moving like a yellow whirlwind, fooled us all until somebody yelled 'Tanks!' Then we noticed some black specks speeding out in front of the dust cloud and the alarm spread like lightning and men all around us dropped everything and raced for their vehicles.

'It's only a few tanks,' somebody shouted, 'it's just Jerry feeling his oats!'

'Only a few. There's dozens of them. Look! It's the whole bloody German army!'

The dust cloud shifted and we suddenly had a clearer view. There must have been at least 200 tanks out there. There were other vehicles too. Motorized infantry, armoured cars, lorries and tank recovery vehicles. The desert seemed to be crammed full of every kind of transport.

With a great roar the tanks around us moved off. We hitched up our guns and pulled out too – just as the shells started to rain down on us. The Germans were obviously trying to take us by surprise and push through at the Bir Hacheim end of the Gazala Line instead of farther north as we had all expected. By throwing in the bulk of their armour here they planned to break through and then swing round in a big arc and cut off the rest of our army. The tanks which went forward to meet them were hopelessly outnumbered. All they could do was fight a last-ditch battle to enable the rest of our troops to re-group and form a new defensive position farther back.

The whole of the Gazala Line erupted into an upheaval of fire, smoke and explosions and many of the British boxes fought out a last-ditch battle before they were swept aside by the advancing German tide. It soon became clear that Rommel was throwing everything he had into an all-out assault to smash through at Gazala and capture Tobruk. He would then be free to continue his advance and push on into Egypt.

We took up a position about 300 yards in front of our other troop of guns. The idea was to fire for as long as we could over open sights and then fall back behind this troop so that they in turn could engage the enemy and then fall back behind us and so on.

The slogging match went on and the thunder of the guns was continuous. We fired point-blank into the dust and smoke and it was really too close for comfort because the splinters ricocheted off the enemy tanks and zipped and whined about us, making us all duck. Soon the desert in front of us became littered with wrecked and burning tanks. The German tank recovery units were out there too, working in the thick of the battle, loading the smashed-up tanks on to their huge trailers and hauling them back to their workshops behind the lines. Those workshop crews were most efficient. If they couldn't put a tank back on to the road again they would make good use out of it, such as removing the gun turret and setting it up in a commanding position somewhere.

The Stukas came over and blasted our positions and this, together with the shelling, caused the sand, already churned up and ground into a fine powder by countless vehicles, to billow up into a thick yellow fog so that we couldn't see the enemy tanks until they were almost upon us. We pulled out of there and fell back behind our other troop but before we could get into action again the shells came crashing down here too. That other troop was practically wiped out. The remnants came racing back – just two trucks, three lorries and only one gun. The other guns had been smashed and their crews were either dead or wounded.

We managed to escape under cover of darkness and if we hadn't got out of there quickly those tanks would really have ironed us out. That night we found ourselves in the middle of a great mass of disorganized and fleeing troops and the chaos was indescribable. During previous battles the Germans had captured huge numbers of British trucks, guns and lorries which they put to good use, and now their forward elements had become so mixed up in this headlong race that many of the vehicles we passed were full of German troops. They drove recklessly with their headlights switched on. We could hear them shouting to each other and singing and the situation could almost be described as comic opera. One or two of our own crew had been drinking up their whisky in case they were captured and they shouted and swore at the Germans but nobody seemed to pay any attention to them. Maybe, in the darkness, the Germans thought they were their own men practising their English on them and trying to be funny. Even if the Germans did recognize us they didn't bother to fire. All they wanted was to get on. No complications. No side battles. No distractions. Maybe they thought that we were already their prisoners and they would sort us all out later. Right now their one aim was to put as much mileage behind them as possible and drive on into Egypt. For our part all we could do was sit tight, light our cigarettes and wave to them in a friendly manner as they passed us.

As this crazy cavalcade raced on through the night it soon became clear to us that unless we could edge out of there and get clear we would, in fact, all find ourselves prisoners of the Boche in the morning. Tubby Wilson realized this too and he raced up in his 15-hundredweight.

'We've got to get out of here,' he yelled, 'I've told the others. When I flash my headlights follow me!'

He drove on ahead and we accelerated after him. The trucks behind us followed suit and even when we left the stream of traffic and drove off into the open desert the Germans did not seem to be bothered about us. We drove all night, bumping across the rough stony desert, heading south-eastward. We knew that sooner or later if we kept going in that direction we would join up with the rest of our Division. However, the next day we were ordered to turn about and after several hours of hard driving we noticed that the desert was criss-crossed with tank tracks – a vast chequerboard which stretched for miles in every direction. We came across hundreds of smoking burnt-out tanks. In every direction as far as you could see the desert was nothing but a tank graveyard!

It was an uncanny business weaving our way through those still smouldering hulks where now only the vultures perched. Eventually we made contact with a red-tabbed staff officer who informed us that, after a tremendous tank battle, the Germans had been halted. Their desperate bid for Egypt after their brief breakthrough at the Gazala Line had failed.

Farther on we met some of the scattered remnants of our own Division and it was here that we had a chance to talk to the tank crews. We learned from one of the commanders, a smoke-begrimed, exhausted looking sergeant, what it was like to be bottled up in a mobile steel box in the middle of a battlefield.

His squadron, which had been operating the Honey type of tank, had recently taken over some of the newly-arrived and much bigger General Grants from America. These tanks were fitted with a 75mm gun in addition to a 37mm and the crew in these big tanks now totalled six men: the commander, the driver, and a gunner and loader for each of the two guns. One of these loaders also acted as wireless operator.

'As you all know those eighty-eights are the devil,' the sergeant said. 'They have this tremendously high velocity. First you hear the shell overhead, then the crash when it bursts followed by the more distant thud of the gun itself. Of course the worst moment in a tank is when you're hit – especially if it's an eighty-eight. There is this almighty clang. The concussion is almost like a blow on the head and the cabin fills with dust and you can't see anything. And just when you think you've got away with it – crash! You're hit again. I tell you, it's just like putting your head up against a cathedral bell when it starts to toll!'

Up in that Gazala Line for instance we were hit by an armour-piercing shell which didn't penetrate. The next one went right through the front and out the back and it took the wireless operator's legs clean off him. Crash! We were hit again and the periscope of the seventy-five was wrecked so all we had was the thirty-seven. The next shot made an even bigger hole in our front, hit the thirty-seven mounting and killed the gunner. We had to reverse out of that fight into some cover behind a ridge of sand.

We managed to fix the spare periscope on to the seventy-five but the stuff was really flying about out there and there was no time to get rid of those two dead men. All we could do was wipe the blood off the instruments and go forward again. I can tell you there was a real mess in that tank!

By then the Squadron Leader's tank had been put out of action so we just had to use our wits and battle it out on our own. As you know a tank can chew up a lot of fuel especially in an action like Gazala when we were up against about two hundred and fifty Mark IIIs and Mark IVs. We were soon scattered all over the place and then we ran out of petrol. We had to sit there, out in the desert, miles from anywhere, and hope one of the petrol lorries would find us!'

'And did it?' I asked him.

'Eventually, yes, but we had to sit there and pretend we had been clobbered while several German tanks went by. With that gaping hole in our front, and our smashed up bodywork and all, we managed to get away with it. It was hot though stuck in there, pretending to be dead as it were, never knowing when one of those passing tanks would send us to Kingdom Come for good. You begin to realize what Cranmer must have felt like when the executioner asked if anybody had a match!'

We moved forward, together with more guns, tanks and infantry into a place called Knightsbridge – so named I believe because a regiment of guards were holding the positions there. Here there was no peace, no stalemate. The Germans had brought up more 88mm guns and hundreds of tanks. We were in action almost continuously and the searing heat and the sand which had been churned up by thousands of vehicles, and which hung about us in thick choking clouds, was probably why our particular stretch of desert became known as the Cauldron.

One evening after we had rigged up the camouflage netting and dug our slit trenches, Buckley came up to me. He knew as well as I did that Tobruk was in dire peril. I had already told him about my association with Mary-Anne and he could see that I was worried.

'Mary-Anne will be alright. The Germans don't harm civilians let alone nurses.'

'Don't they? That lot haven't seen a woman for months and you know what the Boche are like!'

'I know what we Aussies are like too and I reckon she can look after herself!'

I was silent. We were not far from Tobruk and a wild thought suddenly struck me. The road was still open. Maybe I could dash in there with a truck and get her out before it was too late. I mentioned this idea to Buckley because I knew he would stand in for me. If there were any questions he could say that I had gone to see the MO because my arm was playing up. He shook his head.

'Forget it. The MPs would pick you up. They'd put you down as a deserter and with things as they are you wouldn't stand a chance. What the hell use would you be to Mary-Anne then?'

He was right of course and the din of artillery and the constant thunder of tanks going past us reminded me that it was too late to worry now.

Sometimes in the evening when things were less noisy we would sit around and play cards or chat about this and that. Hardly anybody read a book. Maybe this was because any books we'd had had been read ages ago and had either been passed on or lost or used up to light a fire. Once, Doug Walton tried to cheer us up by telling us a story about his grave-digging days.

'I was in charge of a pretty big cemetery and we were always busy. After all, when you think of it, our kind of business really has no end. Often the funeral parlour was stacked with coffins, one on top of the other. Well, as you know there are two kinds of coffin, the cremation coffin and the good old oak lead-lined type with the heavy brasswork which went into the ground. These coffins were stacked in there choc-a-bloc and I remember once when a cremation coffin was taken out and loaded up for burial and an oak coffin sent along to the crematorium!'

'What happened?'

'The cremation coffin was covered with flowers and I don't think anybody noticed except me and I didn't say anything. After all, think of the poor relatives!'

'So the cremation coffin was put into the ground. The wrong man was buried?'

'That's right. Anyway what the hell does it matter? But the boys at the crematorium had a problem. You can't put a lead-lined oak coffin with heavy brass handles and name plates into the furnace because it would jam up the works!'

'What happened?'

'They took the poor man out and shovelled him in as he was!'

Doug Walton shook his head. 'The widow of the chap who was supposed to be cremated wanted his ashes, together with anything else that was left such as his gold teeth and signet ring. She got a load of ashes alright but no gold. They also sent her the photograph of a gorgeous young woman called Betsy which the occupant of the oak coffin had wanted to take with him into eternity!'

Tubby Wilson drove up. 'Prepare to move. Some Jerry tanks have broken through further north!'

'How many?'

'About a hundred.'

'Anybody helping us?'

'I shouldn't think so.'

A hundred tanks! Somehow I felt that our time was running out. Another officer drove up and he and Wilson spread out a map on the bonnet of one of the trucks.

'As you know the Germans tried to come through at Bir Hacheim but they couldn't shift us or those French troops there. My guess is they'll try again but in the meantime we've got to stop them up here or it'll be goodbye Tobruk!'

Mary-Anne! I cursed. They'd ship her off to Germany and I'd never see her again. At that moment I could have taken on those tanks single handed.

'The Germans have got this big momentum going. They're all over the place. They're shooting off their rifles, machine guns, field artillery even their Very lights. Just banging away into the empty desert and trying to make a big noise. They're trying every trick to scare us into thinking they are a mighty force. It's all a big bluff but they've still got an iron fist to back it up with!'

I asked Wilson 'What are our chances? Can we hold Tobruk?' Wilson jerked his thumb into the air. 'I was in a spotter plane yesterday. They've got tanks and eighty-eights, hundreds of them, all over the place.

Tobruk? I'd say it's only a matter of a day or two now!'

We drove into the night, towards the great glow which hung in the sky, towards the roar of thousands of engines and when we stopped to take up our new position the desert seemed to be on fire. It was as if the whole world had come up in arms against us.

About fifty tanks had been rushed to our sector but they stood little chance against the hundred or more German Mark IVs and soon after the battle began the desert was strewn with blazing hulks. The 88s which had been brought up during the night then raked the plain, the squadron headquarters became separated and the remaining tank crews had to fight on their own initiative. We fired over open sights until there was nothing to see except a fog of black smoke. In not much more than thirty minutes all fifty of those tanks were lost. The 88 barrage then lifted and like some devil's blowlamp swept across our gun position and began to search out our wagon lines in the rear.

Later that day we were ordered out of the Gazala Line. Everybody else was pulling out too, getting out of their boxes and destroying their ammunition and petrol dumps. From the coast all the way down to Bir Hacheim the British front line seemed to be collapsing. When the shells started to crash down behind us we knew we were finished. Rommel, as cunning as ever, had broken through at Bir Hacheim and sent his armour round to cut us off in the rear. The road was jam-packed with vehicles, all heading east, all trying to put as much distance as possible between them and the German steamroller and, while the panic grew, they could only travel as fast as the vehicle in front of them which was often a mere crawl.

It was on this road that we came across a truck loaded with goods of almost every description. Looted Italian food and drink, clothing, cigarettes and souvenirs. The vehicle seemed to be a kind of mobile shop and, although the German shells were beginning to catch up on us, I noticed that several other vehicles had pulled in off the road and were parked there. The proprietor, a big fat Cockney, was calling out the odds as if he were back on his stall in Limehouse and doing a brisk trade. I told our driver to keep going but as we passed the 'shop' I was struck by the sign that had been put up there: 'IN GOD WE TRUST, EVERYBODY ELSE – CASH!

That night I think most of us fell asleep on our feet.

Wilson raced up in his truck. 'Destroy your gun. We're going to ditch. The whole Division has been ordered to break out in small mobile units and head west. We'll use the fifteen hundredweights. If we can break through to the west and then head south and then east we might be able to get out that way. Anyway it's our only chance. We have orders to attack the enemy wherever we find him!'

The west was German and Italian occupied territory. It seemed a crazy idea yet it was our only hope. If we could surprise and confuse the enemy by hitting him in his own territory while his armies were going over to the offensive we might, with luck, be able to break through, make our way back in a big sweep round and link up with the rest of our forces. We could hear the rattle and squeel of tank tracks. If we didn't get out of there by morning we'd be mincemeat.

'Get out now!' Wilson ordered. 'Remember, don't go south yet or you'll be caught. Head west. Turn south later and then turn east. The whole Division is doing the same so if you get into trouble you might get some back-up. Anyway, some of us will get through. Good luck!'

Before he drove off I ran across to him. 'Tobruk? What happened over there?'

'Tobruk's gone!'

It was like a slap in the face. Mary-Anne! She was not the sort to run away. At that moment I felt desperate enough to go over to the Germans if only I was sure that I could find her. Then I realized that they'd put me in a prisoner of war camp and I would be worse off than before.

It gave us a strange feeling seeing Wilson drive off like that. Now, we were on our own and we were in a mess. **Until** now we had all been part of a big team and the orders had come down from the Battery Command Post and you knew where you were. Now, we were like a motor without an engine – as if we had to get out and push!

'Come on you lot. You heard what he said. We've got about four hours before first light and we can go a long way in that time!'

We could have blown the gun up but the Germans who were very close would have come down on us so I went off to fetch a sledgehammer. I hated to smash the breech mechanism but I was the Number One and it was up to me to do the dirty work. That gun had served us well and it was like putting down a faithful dog.

We headed out in our 15-hundredweight and almost immediately ran into a big encampment of enemy troops. We drove slowly and carefully with our lights on. The Germans had captured hundreds of British trucks and in the darkness it was almost impossible to tell that we were an enemy. Farther on we found ourselves in the middle of another concentration and this time we were challenged. I knew little German but my crew who were riding in the back shouted back what German they knew but mostly it was gibberish, although I did hear some German swear words. They promptly switched on their searchlights and started shooting at us. I happened to be driving so I put my foot down on the accelerator and yelled at my crew to open up with the Bren gun. We drew a lot of fire and it was scary but we had one big advantage. We could fire in any direction whereas the Germans had to be careful for fear of hitting their own troops.

That little sally, together with the likelihood of scores of other encounters from the rest of our split-up Division, must have startled and confused the Germans into wondering whether the British were trying to launch a last-ditch counter-attack.

We kept going and when daylight came we passed a long line of tanks. Incredibly, our luck held. Maybe it was because most of us, including the Germans,were stripped to the waist in that heat and, unless you looked more closely, you could hardly tell one 'uniform' from another. Once we passed a group of marching men who, seeing that we were travelling away from the front line, waved and jeered at us and pointed in the opposite direction. We waved back and laughed and nothing happened.

We drove on past tanks, guns and infantry columns. Many of them had stopped to cook breakfast and nobody paid any attention to us. Others were doing maintenance work on their vehicles or tanking up for their long journey to the front.

'I can smell a sausage egg and bacon breakfast over there!' Corbett, who was sitting next to me exclaimed. 'How about us going across and joining that queue for a handout?'

I wasn't sure whether he was joking. Corbett was crazy enough for anything. I could smell that aroma too and I drove a little faster. 'Out of the frying pan eh…?'

Later that morning we took a chance and turned south. I had been hoping to see other transport from our Division but there was nothing out there except that endless stretch of shimmering sand. The desert, like the ocean, was vast, empty and just as thirsty.

I decided to ration our water to one pint per day but I soon discovered that this was a mistake. The men kept nipping at their water bottles until by midday there was hardly any water left. In future I would dish out a half pint in the morning and a half pint in the evening.

As we journeyed farther south the desert became a furnace and even at night the rocks were still hot to the touch. And there were the usual mirages – often great sheets of water which receded and then disappeared as you came close. We were used to these tantalizing visions, some of them so realistic that you could swear there was water there. However, we always had to check them out in case, one day, it turned out to be the real thing!

We came across some old tank and lorry tracks and once we found the remains of a German truck. Sandstorms had scoured every scrap of paint to the bare metal. The Bedouin had stripped out the vehicle and they had even taken the wheels off and carted them away. About a mile farther on we found one of the occupants; Just a few bones which the jackals had dragged about. The truck had probably been shot up by aircraft and this man had managed to get clear and struggle on until he died of thirst or wounds.

Every few miles our radiator boiled up and we had to stop to cool the engine and pour in more of our precious water. The heat, the everlasting sand and swarms of flies, and the plain fact that we were lost, began to get the men down so that, in the evening, after the water ration, I encouraged them to talk. They could take it in turns to tell a story, any story, as long as it wasn't about the war.

That evening, while we were having a brew up I told them about Mary-Anne and how her father had found some diamonds in the outback of Australia. It made a good yarn and that drawn look in their faces seemed to ease out a little as they sipped their tea.

'Who's next? What about you Frank? Don't tell us you haven't kicked over the turf for the odd diamond?'

The Australian wiped the sweat from his face and he lit a cigarette.

'As you know I'm a sheep farmer but, since we're on the subject, I reckon I could tell you a thing or two about diamonds. No, I didn't find any in Australia but maybe that was because I was about a thousand miles away from the places you mentioned. I was pretty hard up once and I'd heard that South Africa was the place to look for them things so I took a year off and went over there, to try my luck.'

Buckley took a long pull on his cigarette and left us wondering when all that smoke would stop coming out of his mouth.

'Diamonds? I know a place where anybody with the price of a steamer ticket, time to spare and a little luck thrown in can make a fortune!'

The others perked up. Tired and thirsty though they were this was the sort of thing they could listen to.

'Good eyesight is essential because he has to pick out some rather dull looking things like bits of soapy glass.'

Buckley laughed. 'Out of these things come mink coats and mansions, private yachts and swimming pools, suicide, strokes and murder. Diamonds? Sometimes I wonder whether those stones aren't cursed!'

He told us that this place was a dry, red, mimosa-covered stretch of country not far from the Vaal river in South Africa where, in the old days, acres of land could be bought for a bottle of whisky and later sold for a fortune.

The first South African diamond was discovered by a child in 1866 and used as a plaything. Twenty years later an old prospector named George Walker tripped over an outcrop of rock which was the beginning of the great Rand gold reef. Since that first stone was found, only seventy-six years ago, more than £500,000,000 worth of those bits of 'soapy glass' have come out of the country, not to mention the thousands of millions of pounds taken from the gold mines of the Witwatersrand!

'The child and that poor prospector. If only they could have seen the outcome. The wealth, the happiness, the misery!'

Buckley drained what was left of his tea and stared into his mug.

'Farmers, businessmen, down and outs. All try their luck on the roulette wheel of the Red Velt!'

He told us how he had once journeyed to a sunny little diamond dorp on the Vaal river called Bloemhof.

'One of the prospectors there found a strange black object in one of his final diggings. It looked like a chunk of stinkwood but he soon discovered it was a piece of bort. This stuff is really a rough diamond which is mostly used for industrial purposes and, oddly enough, for testing doubtful stones. A diamond and a bort will scratch anything – except a diamond. If a stone stood up to the scratch test that was the magic moment!'

Buckley described how the digger had a few 'windows' cut in the stone and he was astonished to see a clear green light radiating from its translucent depths. The stone was polished and a beautiful rare diamond was discovered which eventually sold for a vast sum.

Another prospector found a few diamonds on his claim which happened to have more edges on them than usual. He promptly put them into an empty whisky bottle for safe keeping which he carried about with his kit from one digging to another. One day he decided to sell them and discovered they had vanished. Those diamonds had actually eaten their way through the thick glass at the bottom of the whisky bottle. Diamonds can do strange things, but that prospector's faith in whisky was shaken for life by those fierce, heavy little stones!

Buckley told us about the untapped wealth which, to this day, lies along the valley of the Vaal river.

'In the early days it was said that the walls of the mud huts in that area were spattered with diamonds for decorative purposes. Well, there may have been something in that because a large diamond was found, some years ago, embedded in the dried cow dung which lined the walls of a native hut!'

Finally Buckley told us about the Orange river which flows east to west across southern Africa and debouches into the Atlantic at Alexander Bay. He described how hundreds of miles from the coast this mighty stream plunges over a precipice before surging through a series of inaccessible canyons on its journey to the sea.

'This wild and lonely place is called the Aughrabies Falls. The Vaal river flows through the richest diamond bearing land in the world before it joins the Orange river, and because diamonds are very heavy stones, who can say that, over the ages, chunks of diamond-bearing rock have not been swept over those falls to sink to the bottom and become embedded, layer upon layer, and ton upon ton? Old farmers and prospectors still believe that if the Orange river could be dammed or diverted and access made to the very foot of this precipice – a bulldozer would be needed to move the diamonds that could be found there!'

Buckley reached across and refilled his mug with tea.

'The rate this war's going it looks as if we'll all end up in South Africa one of these days. So take a stroll yourselves along the red veldt by the Vaal river. Take a spade too. Or if your time's precious, take a header into the Aughbaries Falls. Who knows? You might just come up with a fistful of diamonds!'

CHAPTER NINE

Today we had to make a decision. Should we boil away any more of our precious water or abandon the truck and walk? Either way it didn't seem to make much difference. If we kept on driving our total water supply would vanish by tomorrow evening. If we were on foot we would have enough water to last us for about three days. We chose to walk. Life, as ever, was the big draw even if it was for only a couple more days or so.

We drove on until what water was left in the radiator had boiled away and the engine had seized. We hated to leave the truck. Somehow, that vehicle was all that stood between us and the world we had left behind. Leaving that truck, together with our personal possessions, was a bit of a wrench. As we climbed down, finally, and prepared to set off into the desert, it seemed to be just another routine exercise, and it was difficult to believe that, unless we found water in the next few days,,we would all be dead.

McAlister had once salvaged a gramophone together with some records from the wreck of a German truck. Somehow he had managed to secrete this away and keep it stowed in the various trucks we had been driving since then. Of course, he was loathe to part with it now. He brought it out, put on a record and wound it up and we trudged away from there to the tune of Lili Marlene!

Our direction was north-east. Sooner or later, if we kept going, we would spot something even if it was the enemy. We knew too that the 'powers to be' would hardly allow a whole Division to split up without sending out planes to look for them and if they spotted our truck back there they would only have to make one or two sweeps across the desert to find us too.

That fiery furnace seemed to squeeze the moisture out of us like a sponge and I began to wonder which of us would be the first to drop out. I was sure that, as well as myself, Buckley and McAlister would last the longest. Then again Corbett with his huge Geordie frame might beat us all. On the other hand he had been a drinker. Would a lifetime of alcohol be enough to topple him now?

As it turned out, Rule the wiry Welshman was the first to succumb. He sat down and refused to go on. I believe his recent misdemeanours had been preying on his mind because he told me that God's punishment was about to be visited upon him here in the desert. He was doomed, he said, to die of thirst and go to Hell! I pulled him to his feet and pushed him out in front.

'It's hotter than Hell here anyway, so now's your chance to get used to it!'

We travelled during the day in the hope of being seen by any aircraft that might be out looking for us. The desert was featureless. There were no plants, not even camelthorn. Here the mighty Sahara, devoid of all life, seemed to level out into an eternity of sand.

The gravedigger was the next to show signs of collapse. 'Drop dead here,' I told him, 'and you'll have to bury yourself!' I cut the water ration still further. Rule, who had been staggering on, bent double, as if burdened by the weight of his own cross, dropped out finally. We couldn't drag him along so it looked as if we'd have to leave him there. McAlister went up to him and nodded at his rifle.

'Don't forget if it comes to it, you've still got your best friend!'

Rule shook his head. Suddenly he had lost all his sun tan. He looked scared.

'I'll go to Hell!' he muttered.

'Maybe,' McAlister said, 'but I reckon you'll be alright. You've been a churchgoer. At least you've got some fire insurance behind you!'

'Never mind all that,' I butted in. 'Rule's going to be alright. We're heading in the right direction and we'll soon find some of our own troops and then we'll send back a rescue party to pick him up!'

I knew it was all talk. Who on earth would we meet in two or three days out in this wilderness? We might as well be adrift on a raft in the middle of the Pacific Ocean. We clubbed together and left Rule a pint and a half of water. Then I tore off my vest, tied it to the end of his rifle and stuck it in the sand next to him.

'Mother...' I heard Rule mutter as we left him there.

I tried to picture his mother. A little Welshwoman waiting for the postman to bring her another letter from her soldier son? Oh well, at least she would never know how much he had wandered from the straight and narrow!

'Oh should I drown in the deepest of seas

I know whose tears would come down to me....'

Another six miles and Doug Walton collapsed. We managed to get him to his feet but we hadn't the strength to keep him there and when he collapsed finally he said:

'Leave me here. This is the best place. At least I'll have cheated those stinking cemeteries!'

I could tell that he was genuinely glad to have all this space to himself.

We made him as comfortable as possible and left him the same amount of water as we had left Rule. An evening star was beginning to twinkle as we marched away. I knew that if we met anybody they'd have a poor chance of finding those two men back there so I had been tearing up what paper we had in order to leave some sort of trail. It was probably a waste of time but it had been hot and still with no wind to blow the pieces away.

We were anxious to put on a last spurt before running out of water so we travelled for most of that night too. Next day we continued to tear up our bits of paper until we ran out. I then started on my most precious possession – an old letter from Mary-Anne. Ah well, it would be nice if her letter would help to save a dying man. The only thing I didn't tear up was her photograph – that and the London address she had scribbled down for me on a scrap of paper. I'd have kept those things if it had cost a dozen men.

Soon after midday we noticed something dark moving across the desert towards us and at first we thought it was a dust cloud. Then McAlister pointed out that there was no wind. The sun flashed and the object, quivering in the heat like a jelly, resolved itself into a truck. Our spirits fell when we realized that it was German. But beggars cannot be choosers and we would have been glad to see anything even if it had been the devil himself.

There were two men in the truck, a corporal and a private, and, strangely enough they didn't point any weapons at us or attempt to capture us. In fact they were quite friendly and gave us all the water we could drink and told us to climb on board. It turned out that they were lost too. They had become separated from their unit during the

Gazala battle and, like us, were heading north-east because that was where their army lay.

I tried to get them to drive back along my paperchase trail but the corporal said no. Petrol was short and their duty lay in finding their own unit before they got themselves into any more trouble.

The desert here was so flat that we could sometimes travel at 40 mph and it soon became apparent that, if we hadn't met those men, we would all have died of thirst back there. It was a little disturbing though, not knowing which of us would eventually end up as prisoners of war. The two Germans didn't seem to care. They had had enough of the war anyway and if they were taken prisoner then at least they would not have to answer awkward questions from their commanding officer.

A plane swept low, making us duck. A Blenheim probably out looking for men of our own Division. The plane came round again and we suddenly realized that we could be blasted off the desert. The driver stopped the truck, jumped down and started to wave a white handkerchief. The other German did the same and we thought it was a good idea too. It was scary though, zooming over us like that but for some reason they didn't open fire. Maybe they were out of ammunition or didn't want to waste it on a dirty old truck, or they thought we were British driving a captured enemy vehicle. Perhaps it was because we were all waving white handkerchiefs. At any rate the plane flew off and we could only hope that they had radioed our position and that sooner or later a patrol would come out to investigate.

The next day we ran out of petrol. All we could see was that eye-aching stretch of desert. We might as well have been left on a sinking ship. The only difference between that and our ocean of sand was that we wouldn't have to swim for it.

The Germans had salvaged plenty of food and water from their truck, so we were able to keep going on foot. One morning the silence was shattered by the sound of battle and, after climbing a ridge of sand, we spotted one of our field guns shelling a German Mark IV tank. I called the two Germans over.

'There you are. Civilization. We've made it!' I pointed to the tank. 'That's your lot. Ours are over there. Couldn't be more convenient!'

We shook hands, exchanged addresses and swore that we would look each other up after the war. The two Germans headed for the tank while we set off for the field gun.

'A few more minutes and we'll be doing our best to kill each other!' Corbett said as he gave them a final wave.

That gun crew told us that the Eighth Army had been pushed right back to a place called El Alamein.

'El what?'

'El Alamein.'

'Where's that?'

'It's a dirty little one-horse railway halt on the line to Matruh. This whole area is called the Alamein Line.'

They told us that the new front stretched for forty-five miles from the coast to the Qattara Depression.

'Alexandria is only sixty miles from here. One more break through and that's it. They'd be in Cairo too!'

Corbett gave a low whistle. 'Suez, the whole bloody Delta will have gone down the drain!'

Apparently we had been travelling much farther east than we had thought. We learned that while we had been away the Germans had launched repeated attacks and that, more recently, there had been a savage tank battle at Alam el Halfa in their all-out effort to break through at Alamein.

We eventually found what was left of our regiment. They had been badly smashed up and were now being refitted on the Smoha Race Course in Alexandria.

The town was almost in a state of siege. Rumours were going round that the Germans would arrive at any moment and the road to Cairo was jam-packed with vehicles of every description. A battery of guns was followed by long columns of motorized infantry. Then tanks, crushing and chewing up the already broken ribbon of road and behind the tanks a line of trucks and lorries stretching back as far as the eye could see. A choking pall of exhaust fumes and dust enveloped the road.

Units were being ordered back to form the Delta Line – a last-ditch effort to save the Suez Canal. Smoke from GHQ in Cairo stood high above the city as huge quantities of papers were burnt. King Farouk had already left the country in his yacht and the Egyptians were getting ready to hang out their swastika flags. Rommel, it was said, had already ordered Shepheards to reserve him a table.

But it never happened. The Germans ran short of petrol. Their lines of communication stretched back for hundreds of miles into Libya whereas we had only a short distance to go. They never received any of the supplies or reinforcements they had urgently asked for. Every priority was given to the Russian front. In a week or two the threat was over and the Alamein Line had become too strong for the Germans to break.

We did what we could for Walton and Rule and a plane was sent out to look for them, but the desert is a big place and they were never found. Somewhere out there they lie in what Doug Walton had called 'the best place'. I still felt pretty rough after what we had been through – that and losing Mary-Anne – and there were times when I believe I envied him that place of his beneath the stars.

We were granted leave, Corbett, Buckley, McAlister and myself. I wanted to stay in Alex. Cairo had too many memories for me but in the end they persuaded me to go with them. I discovered that the city had changed. Thousands of troops of different nationalities roamed the streets and it had lost any character it might have had. The Tipperary Club was much too crowded and that lovely old piano was out of tune. There were even more beggars on the streets and the shoeshine boys wouldn't leave you alone. They'd follow and pester you for miles and if you refused to have your boots cleaned they'd throw the liquid blacking all over your trousers. I couldn't help feeling that if the Germans did break through they'd soon sort out Cairo and put a little order into the place. I made my way to the hospital just in case, by some miracle, Mary-Anne had got away from Tobruk.

The matron was dark, middle-aged and very pretty.

'Are you the Sergeant she used to talk about? Mike Johnstone? The Sergeant in the field artillery?'

'Yes.'

I told her about my friendship with Mary-Anne and how I had managed to visit her in Tobruk and when I asked her if she had any news of her she shook her head.

'I'm afraid it looks as if she is a prisoner of war.'

I thanked her and gave her the address of my unit in case there was any news. I was about to leave when she called me back.

'We used to work together, Mary-Anne and I,' she said, 'and we used to chat about things. She once told me that you were the only person who really meant anything to her. I do hope you find her.'

We stayed at the New Zealand Club. Buckley and I seemed to tag along together while Corbett and McAlister went off on their own. There was nothing much to do in Cairo. I tried to avoid the Pyramids and the park and those places which Mary-Anne and I used to frequent. We drank a lot and visited the cabarets and went to cool off a little in the air-conditioned metro cinema.

I was glad to get away from Cairo with its flies, stinking streets and beggars. Alex was a little cleaner and at least you'd get a sea breeze there occasionally. I had only been back a couple of days when Tubby Wilson sent for me.

'You're going back to Cairo. You've been detailed to escort a prisoner to Kasr el Nil Barracks.'

That really fed me up. Cairo, the heat and all that filth again. I'd sooner be back in the desert.

'I'd have sent somebody else but you were the only NCO available. The others are away on a forty-eight hour gunnery course.'

'Who is he sir and what did he do?'

'Man called Oates. I haven't actually seen him myself. He's a gunner.

Not our crowd thank goodness. He went absent without leave up in the blue. The idiot had to choose a time like this. He was picked up by the Red Caps on the way to Cairo.'

'That's desertion, isn't it?'

'If that isn't I don't know what is. Poor sod. Probably had too much of it. Wouldn't like to be in his shoes though.'

'Can't the Red Caps do their own dirty work sir?'

'They can't spare any men. They're all out on the roads trying to sort out this chaos. We're the nearest gunner unit, so we've been given the job.'

He could tell that I didn't want to go.

'Look, take your time down there. Enjoy yourself. Nobody's going to say anything if you arrive back here a little late!'

'Frankly, I'd rather be up in the blue.'

'We'll be getting plenty of that again. Soon as we're up to strength we're going into the line at El Alamein.'

Wilson handed me a bulky envelope. 'Because of the chaotic state of the roads we have not attempted to send a dispatch rider with this commitment order. You'll have to deliver the documents yourself together with the prisoner. Clear?'

'Where is the prisoner sir?'

'In the guardhouse. You'll be armed, of course, and if the prisoner attempts to escape, well, you know what King's Regulations have to say about that! As I said, take your time down there. It may be your last chance to see the place again.'

'I shall not be able to get back quick enough. Cairo's a dump!'

I had pictured Oates as a no good slacker type and I was pleasantly surprised when I met him. He was a west countryman, squarely built with good features and he had a ready smile in spite of his predicament. All the same I was fed up. I had just got back from Cairo and I thought I was well rid of the place. I decided to get things clear from the start.

'My name's Johnston and I'm taking you down to Kasr el Nil. If you try and escape,' I tapped my rifle, 'you know what I'm supposed to do!'

Oates gave a short laugh. 'Maybe you'll have better luck than the Germans then.'

A truck had been allocated for us, together with an RASC driver and we drove down to Cairo. After chatting with Oates I realized that he was no coward and I wondered what on earth had made him go absent without leave while still in the front line.

'Do you realize you could be charged with desertion in the face of the enemy?'

'We had been up and down in the desert for months and hardly any of us had had any leave. Things were quiet and I thought I'd take a couple of days off in Cairo, that's all.'

'What, all that way, just for a couple of days? It was a girl wasn't it?'

'Yes.'

'What does she do?'

'She's a nurse at the hospital there.'

My stomach gave a lurch. First Rod and now it was Oates! Somehow I had imagined that I was the only one who had had any luck with the nurses down there. 'We met about three months ago when I had a bit of shrapnel taken out of my leg.'

'So you were wounded. Don't forget to tell them that, it might help at your trial.'

I told him about Mary-Anne. 'She worked at that hospital too. She was captured in Tobruk. She's probably a prisoner of war in Germany by now.'

'More likely they'd put her to work in Italy.'

I hoped he was right. She'd be safe from the bombing there. I couldn't help feeling sorry for Oates. He had got himself into a mess. In peacetime he'd probably have done a short spell in the glasshouse. I didn't like his chances now – particularly after the Germans had got us on the run. The Courts Martial would probably want to make an example of him.

'Waterloo Bridge' was showing at the Cairo Metro so I thought I'd give Oates a last treat and take him along. The driver wanted to see it too so we sat in the back row with Oates between us. After the show I offered to take him up to the hospital so that he could say goodbye to his girl but he shook his head.

'Let her think I'm still up in the blue – you know, soldiering on and all that!'

We drove out of Cairo into the desert. The detention centre was a dreary collection of wooden huts surrounded by tall fences of barbed wire. The guards were yelling at a squad of men who were doubling about with full equipment.

I told the driver to stop just short of the gates. I had all the papers, but what had been nagging at me all the way down from Alex was the fact that, until I handed the prisoner over, the camp authorities knew absolutely nothing about him. Because of the administrative chaos caused by the Eighth Army's retreat to the Alamein Line, I had been appointed sole bearer of the commitment papers as well as escort to the prisoner. In the short time we had been together I had grown to like Oates and that was why I hesitated now. How could I send this poor blighter into a hole like this? A military policeman, the peak of his red cap pulled low over his face, came out of the guardhouse.

'Get the hell out of here!' I told the driver.

The RASC man, startled, looked round at me.

'Quick get out of here' I hissed.

He switched on the ignition but the truck wouldn't start. Maybe the carburettor was flooded or the appalling heat had something to do with it. The engine turned over until it groaned.

'What are you lot doing here?' the MP shouted.

'There's something wrong with the engine so we came out here to give it a run,' I called back.

As soon as I said it I realized what I could be letting myself in for and Oates, who was looking quite pale, must have thought I'd gone off my head. I climbed down and opened up the bonnet and the driver' puzzled, sat there frowning. I was bending over the engine, pretending to adjust something when the MP came up behind me.

I straightened up. 'Could you help us with a push, mate?'

The driver, leaning out of his cab, was quick to catch on. He was a Bolshie Cockney type and only too glad to put one over the hated military police. He whispered something to Oates who climbed down and stood beside me. The driver then released the hand brake and told us to push. The MP stepped forward grudgingly and put his shoulder to the truck with Oates and myself.

The engine coughed, spluttered and sprang into life. The truck ran on down the road leaving Oates, the policeman and myself gasping for breath. I thought the driver was going to carry on and leave us there but he stopped finally, revving the engine furiously. Oates and I then sprinted after him and scrambled on board. When I looked back the policeman, his face red and perspiring, was brushing down his clothes and I could tell by the way he kept staring at us that he was wondering what we were really doing out there.

Oates, who must have wondered whether he had just woken up from a nightmare asked me why I had done it.

'I don't know. Maybe because I wouldn't put my worst enemy in a dump like that. Maybe because I once had a girl in Cairo, too!'

I told the driver to keep going anywhere, while I tried to think. The problem now was what to do with him. I couldn't just drop him off in Cairo and let him get on with it. We had been driving around the outskirts of Cairo for miles when an idea came to me. It seemed crazy enough but I thought it might work.

I was quite friendly with the Sergeant in our battery office, a man called Baker. There was chaos in the desert and disorganized columns of troops were streaming back from the front. Suppose I could get Baker to put Oates on to the strength of my own unit? With all those battered and mixed-up regiments who would question the addition of one more man, and a gunner at that, to the Battery list? My best card of all was the fact that Tubby Wilson had not even seen Oates. Better than turning him loose in Cairo where, without money or anywhere to go, he would very soon be picked up by the MPs. If Baker refused then I would just have to send him away and let him take his chances. If Tubby Wilson questioned me I would tell him that I had deposited Oates at the detention centre and then hope that, with the intense activity going on everywhere, we would quickly move back into the line and that everything would blow over and be forgotten.

I liked the RASC man and I knew, somehow, that he would never betray me so I took him into my confidence when I told Oates about my plan. Oates of course was so relieved at any chance of avoiding prison, or worse, that he swore that he would forever be in my debt.

When we arrived back in Alex we said goodbye to the RASC man who shook hands with Oates and gave him the address of his unit. He told him that if things went wrong.and if there was anything he could do to help, he would be very happy to oblige.

I gave Oates some money and left him in the canteen while I went in search of Sergeant Baker. I had to be careful. If I told him that I had not only failed to deliver the prisoner but actually planned to set him loose he wouldn't have dared to help me, good friend though he was. I found Baker behind his typewriter in the Battery office. We hadn't seen each other for some time and after chatting about this and that I brought the conversation round to Oates.

'Look old chap, this poor blighter's unit was blown to bits. I picked him up in the blue and gave him a lift to the transit camp here. He doesn't want to go back to the RA Depot at Almaza. He hates that place. He's a good man to have in any unit. Do you think you could type him on to our strength?'

'You must be crazy. I could end up in the can. Has he got any papers?'

'They're up in the blue somewhere with the rest of his kit but I expect they'll turn up one day.'

I told Baker about the hundreds of other men who had also lost their units and who, because of the emergency, were being taken on to the strength of different regiments.

'I'm short of two men on my own gun as you know. This man Bates is a good chap. He was with the Third RHA.'

'The Third RHA,' Baker exclaimed. 'That was a crack unit. Right of the line and all that! Well, alright then, seeing he's a pal of yours I'll make out the necessary returns and he can join us today. As far as I am concerned Bates has been sent up here from Almaza as a replacement. Remember, not a word to anybody about this OK?'

I told Baker that it was definitely OK.

And that was how Gunner Oates, wanted by the military police for 'desertion' in the field, came to be a member of my gun team.

CHAPTER TEN

The Battle of Alamein opened up at 9.40 pm on 23 October 1942 with a barrage of a thousand guns. Our gun was one of those which tore the night sky into shreds, so I suppose you could say that we played a one thousandth part of that night's work. From north to south the desert seemed to explode as thousands of shells burst among the enemy positions and the tremendous din sent our 25-pounder gun jigging about on the sand. As the evening wore on the thunder of artillery increased until we wondered how anything could still exist in that cataclysmic vortex out there in front of us. We fired until the barrel of our gun became too hot; until the threat of a premature burst was an ever-present sweat. We were lucky. Maybe it was because the shells we rammed home didn't stay in the breech long enough for that to happen.

The barrage rose to a massive drumming until it seemed that the whole of Egypt was being broken up by pneumatic drills. The sheer din was exhilarating and we shouted and sang. We were taking part in one of the biggest battles of the war. We were making history.

But we knew that we wouldn't get away with it. The enemy had hundreds of guns over there too and soon enough their shells came banging over as they searched us out. And there was nothing we could do about it. We had a schedule to work out and we couldn't run for shelter or dive into our slit trenches. We could only duck and wince and hope that those flying shards of steel would miss us.

We all knew that this could be the last big throw in North Africa. The British had been pouring arms and equipment into the country for months, we now had about 800 tanks many of which were newly-arrived American Sherman and General Grants. The Germans, short of petrol, and whose lines of communication stretched back for hundreds of miles could only muster about 270 tanks and, when the big attack came, Rommel was on sick leave in Germany.

The Germans fought for every inch of ground while Rommel flew back to try and save what was left of his army. The Germans, in spite of our devastating bombardment, held their positions for twelve days and it was during this time that Hitler issued his 'victory or death' order. We knew then that things were going to get rough.

We fired night and day, and we had to use our precious water to cool down the barrel, but the Germans were still there. They even counter-attacked with a massive artillery barrage and then threw in tanks. Somehow they knew that this was it. If they couldn't beat the British here they'd never get to Cairo and see the Pyramids.

Besides Oates we had taken on another man, Shipley, to make up our crew of six. Shipley, too, had been in it from the beginning. His battery had been shot to pieces at Alam Halfa and he had been posted straight on to us. Bill Shipley was a hard-drinking taciturn regular who had seen service in India before the war. Come to think of it we were all hard drinkers, especially McAlister and Corbett, but Shipley carried enough liquor in his kitbag to start a mirage.

We got a big surprise when he pulled off his shirt. His chest was tattooed with a great bounding tiger, his back presented us with an impressive looking Chinese dragon while on each of his arms was a slim and beautiful dancing girl. By flexing his muscles he could bring the tiger or the dragon to life. He could make the girls smile, dance or do almost anything he wanted. You had to hand it to him. The whole job was a work of art!

I had the nagging feeling that sooner or later somebody would find out about Oates but the days went by and we hammered away at the German positions and no questions were asked. It certainly looked as if nobody was going to bother you if you were in the front line.

Oates proved to be a good man. Once at Alamein when our guns were spaced at only thirty yards apart Number Two gun received a near hit. I sent Oates and Corbett across to give them a hand. Two of the crew had been blown to pieces and two were badly wounded. With the help of the remaining crew members they got that gun back into action in time to knock out a German Mark IV tank which suddenly appeared out of a smokescreen.

Ten more enemy tanks appeared out of that smoke, moving across the desert as if in review order. I noticed that Oates had taken the layer's job while Corbett was putting on the range. The other two men were slamming shells into the breech and getting them off quicker than anything I had seen at Aldershot Tattoo. Much depended on Oates but he was a good layer because I just had time to see the turret of the leading tank fly off, leaving its gun sagging like a bent poker.

We were pretty busy too and a big problem was the hard stony ground. The trail would not dig in and every time we fired the recoil sent the gun charging back several feet and we had to dodge out of the way to avoid serious injury.

Over on our left some German infantry, Panzer Grenadiers who had been following up behind the tanks, made a dash for Number Four gun. They shot down the crew but our own infantry who had been moving up among the rocks caught them with a burst of machine-gun fire. Our troop captain together with a couple of signallers then worked their way close and manned the gun themselves. Another wave of enemy infantry got within a hundred yards.

'Crash!' A shell from Number Four gun smashed into the charging men pointblank and the machine gun finished then off. The captain and his two signallers worked that gun like demons. Like the rest of us they couldn't get out even if they had been ordered to. The Germans were all over the place. Suddenly hundreds of men who had been advancing under cover of the dust and smoke appeared in front of us. Behind them came tanks. We depressed the barrel of our gun and, aiming at the tanks, cut wide swathes through those charging men. The desert became littered with the dead and dying and the tanks ran straight over them.

One of the tanks headed for Number Two gun, clearly intending to run it down. Corbett snatched up a grenade and dashed forward, trying to get into the dead angle of the tank's machine gun. He jumped up on to the steel monster, pulled the pin of his grenade and thrust it down the gun barrel, then he leapt away. There was a flash and a tremendous explosion. The grenade had set off a shell which was still in the breech. The front of that tank was blown wide open. There was just a big jagged hole out of which the fire roared like a flame-thrower!

Corbett had resumed his post on Number Two gun when a tank stopped close by to get its bearings. He grabbed another grenade, raced across and wedged it into one of the tracks beneath the caterpillar guard. The tank lurched forward. Another explosion and the massive steel tracks spun away from the tank like a runaway serpent. Corbett raced back to Number Two gun and cranked down the barrel until it was pointing, like a finger of doom, at the crippled tank. The tank's gun turret swung round and both guns fired simultaneously.

I don't think two shells ever came closer to a head-on bust up. The tank shell exploded in front of Number Two gun blowing the gun over and killing the remaining two members of its original crew. Oates and Corbett were lucky. When they pulled the gun up the sights were smashed, the barrel bent and the steel shield twisted out of shape like cardboard. Then the tank, which had received a direct hit, burst into flames and Corbett and Oates ran for their lives, we saw the danger too and dived for what cover we could find. The tank, loaded with ammunition, blew up like a landmine.

We fired so many shells that day I thought the barrel would melt. Behind us we could hear the thudding of mortars and the rattle of machine-gun fire. The infantry were having a go too, but they couldn't get any closer to the enemy or they would run into our own shellfire.

I don't think any gun, out of that thousand, had a better crew than mine. Corbett and Oates had now rejoined us and I had a full team again. The crews of Numbers Two and Four guns had been wiped out and I began to wonder how our own luck would hold. How many 'Alameins' would we have to fight before we beat the Germans for good? In those late October days of 1942 it was a sobering thought.

I was glad that I'd taken on Oates and got him out of that mess. In the short time he had been with us he had proved that he was no coward. Shipley, too, was a good man and as I watched him now, stripped to the waist and covered in dirt I had to smile. That tiger of his, more fearsome than ever, seemed about to spring out at us. The dragon, too, was a frightful sight and the dust and sweat on the dancing girls had turned them into a couple of witches.

Over to the left I could hear a lot of yelling and small-arms fire and through the fog of dust and smoke I could just make out Number Three gun. A German assault group had charged the gun and killed two of the crew and the others were battling it out with spades, pickaxes and rifle butts.

Our next shell ripped the tracks off another tank. The gun turret swung round and the shells, bursting on the granite-hard ground, sent steel, sand and chunks of rock whizzing about us. We were using armour-piercing and one of our shots went clean through the side of the tank into the control cabin and ricocheted about in there with a din that would live with me for ever. As Buckley remarked afterwards, the crew would hardly have been worth burying. They would have had to be scraped off the walls of the cabin.

The tanks dispersed while the German commander wondered how to deal with this dangerous enemy among the rocks. We could see a recce car racing about and not long afterwards a Stuka roared overhead but its bombs missed us and whistled down among the wagon lines. Then the 88s started up on us.

The front line seemed to be all over the place but slowly we punched our way forward. Ahead our planes were blasting a minefield. Then the artillery had a go. Finally the engineers went in to clear a lane through. We had hitched up the gun and had driven through the lane when twenty German Mark IVs came out of the smoke like phantoms. There was no time to unhook our gun and get into action and Buckley who was driving simply put his foot down on the accelerator. Our own infantry were all round us, running behind our vehicles to try and get some protection from the sheeting bullets. The enemy command tank ran into soft sand which had been churned up by the shelling and the engine whined as the driver engaged first gear. The infantry were a pretty rough lot, a northern crowd I think, probably Geordies, and one of these men ran forward and climbed up on to the tank. He pulled the partly-open hatch wide, removed the pin of his grenade, waited a couple of seconds, then dropped his bomb inside and leaped away. Crash! The hatch cover flew off, smashed his head open and scattered his brains over the side of the tank. Still in first gear, the tank heaved itself out of the sand and crept away, pilotless, to the rear. Almost every weapon we had seemed to take it on but the tank kept going for half a mile before one of our medium guns finished it off.

The following tank stopped and the hatch opened. The commander who wanted to see what was happening was immediately struck by machine-gun fire and slid back into the cabin. One of the infantrymen ran up behind the tank and lobbed a grenade into the still-open hatch but a quick-thinking crew member picked it up and threw it back. The bomb burst just below the gun turret and blew off half the gun barrel.

Then we were past, driving all out across the desert, leaving those tanks for our aircraft or for our heavier guns to finish off. Hundreds of men and vehicles were spilling out across the desert. The British army seemed to be in a headlong race forward.

We stopped to cool the engine. All around us lay the bodies of men who had been killed during the past few months. Dried out, mummified, their uniforms bleached almost white by the sun, it was difficult to believe that these were once men who had lived and breathed.

The past forty-eight hours had also seen some heavy fighting near here. Close by stood an infantry brigade's headquarters truck with its signals truck, a cook wagon and an ambulance. Men, separated from their units, stood about. We watched a stretcher case arrive. Chest and stomach wounds. The only survivor of his battalion. There had been bayonet fighting and a wadi had changed hands several times. The wounded man reports on the German positions and then dies. His battalion is wiped out. A Brigade Major climbs down from his truck and addresses a young Captain,

'Where is your Company?'

The Captain, filthy and trembling, points to where forty-five bedraggled looking men are lining up at the field kitchen.

Earlier that day that same kitchen staff had found themselves in a savage hand-to-hand battle with a party of Germans. The chief cook had fought them off with a carving knife while his assistant had attacked them with a heavy iron frying pan and then heaved a pot of boiling water over them. It was the same when the Headquarters office had been overrun. The clerks had fought with spiked files and paper knives and they had even thrown their typewriters at the Germans.

We drove on westward. The sun was obliterated by the clouds of fine yellow dust which clung to our clothes and skin and which got under the bonnet and put engines out of action. We breathed so much of that stuff in that I wondered our lungs didn't seize up too. We were all desperately thirsty but the warm sandy liquid in our waterbottles only seemed to make things worse. We were hungry too.

Before the attack began the MO had advised us not to eat anything. Then, if anybody had a stomach wound they would stand a better chance of survival. Even a couple of biscuits, he had told us, could aggravate a stomach wound and cause internal bleeding. After a while most of us took a chance and passed the tin opener round.

We came up against more minefields and acres of barbed wire. The Germans were not going to let us through easily. There was no cover and the hundreds of vehicles spread out across the desert were sitting ducks for the odd Stuka. Once, when the water wagon was parked a short distance away, we were able to cadge a little extra water and wash some clothes. I had hung my washing out to dry when a machine gun opened up from beyond a minefield and ripped it into shreds. I had left that scrap of paper with Mary-Anne's address in one of my pockets and I could see it now, fluttering onto the minefield. There was nothing I could do for if I tried to retrieve it either the machine gun would get me or I would be blown up on the minefield. I felt really bitter for in losing that scrap of paper I had lost all contact with Mary-Anne.

That evening under cover of darkness we un-hooked our guns and lined them up on the minefield and machine-gun emplacements in front of us.

Tomorrow at dawn we were to blast a way through so that our tanks and infantry could follow up. We were so close we could hear the Germans talking to each other. If they had spotted us there they must have thought we were one of their own outfits. Apart from the odd flare it was pretty quiet and farther on down the line we could hear somebody singing 'Lili Marlene' to the accompaniment of a mouth organ, we spoke in whispers and anybody who snored or cried out in their sleep was not allowed to get their heads down. Hardly any of us slept anyway. You don't feel like dropping off when the enemy is just a stone's throw away. Worst of all we were not allowed to smoke but any old sweat knew how to cope with that.

The sunrise waa breathtaking and had it not been behind us I believe that its sheer beauty would have been distracting. Soon it was light enough to train the muzzle of our gun on to the bunkers opposite.

Ten seconds. Five. Four. Three. Two... 'Fire!'

The guns tore that beautiful dawn sky into shreds. There was so much dust and smoke that at first we couldn't see where our shells were landing but it was all a point-blank business so it didn't really matter. We heard the squeel and rattle of caterpillar tracks as thirty Mark IVs came weaving in and out of the smoke and we had to crank down the barrel until our shells were practically skimming the surface of the desert. We would have been overrun if some of our own tanks had not arrived to take part in the battle. Later that day when the enemy positions had been cleared and we went forward the sand around those bunkers was stained red.

Oates had always been a rather quiet type but he had been particularly silent lately and I put it down to a spot of Gypo tummy or something like that and advised him to go sick but he refused. I could understand. You had to have a pretty good reason for reporting sick in the front line, which was probably why many of the men hung on until they were very sick. Nobody wanted to be suspected of malingering with a view to getting away from the danger zone.

We came up against a group of diehard Panzer Grenadiers – Rommel's last-ditch rearguard troops whose orders were to hold up the British advance whatever the cost. I counted forty German Mark IIIs and Mark IVs sitting out there in front of us and the tannoy came to life again with that same old urgency:

'Tanks, gunfire, gun control…!'

I wondered how long our luck would hold. Like throwing dice you can't keep winning all the time. And Oates was bothering me too. He was definitely not himself. He was stumbling about and getting in everybody's way and everytime the gun fired he put his hands over his ears – a thing none of us had bothered to do since our very early days. Eventually I told him to go and lie down at the back somewhere. We knocked out a couple of tanks and then the Germans put down a smokescreen. The Battery Commander's truck came racing up and Lieutenant Hodgson, a man I thoroughly disliked, jumped down.

'Those tanks are holding everything up so we've got to find them and finish them off. We're going to set up an OP out there. Now this is the position. One of our signallers has been killed. You've still got a full crew so I'm taking one of your men to help run out a line.'

We were still in action and I needed all my men so I could only think of Oates. He had once had some training in signals work and it would get him away from the everlasting din and the change might do him good. He was sitting on a box of ammunition staring blankly in front of him when Hodgson and I came up to him. The Lieutenant was in a thoroughly bad temper and, to make matters worse, Oates didn't even bother to get up.

'What the hell…'

'He's been having a spot of Gypo tummy, sir. I told him he could have a rest.'

I could tell already that Hodgson suspected Oates of slacking. I informed him that Oates had had some training in signals work when he was with the RHA.

The Lieutenant ordered Oates into the truck. 'He won't be able to sit around where we're going!'

Like everybody else I was anxious for news.

'What's happening sir?'

'They're pulling out. They're trying to keep their army intact, so they are leaving strong rearguard battalions behind to hold us up. They're short of petrol, guns and tanks but they won't give up easily – not after everything they've put into North Africa, we may have got them on the run but it's going to be a pretty tough slog still!'

He climbed into his truck and, with Oates sitting miserably next to him, drove off.

Hodgson seemed to be a long time setting up his OP and when the orders did come down to us those tanks were at extreme range and we couldn't do much more than speed them on their way. The days passed while we went in and out of action but it was mostly harassing fire on the retreating enemy columns. I had been so busy that I had forgotten about Oates and when he didn't come back to us I thought he must have gone sick and been sent to hospital. Once during a lull in the fighting Hodgson sent for me.

'It's about Gunner Oates. We're holding him on a charge of cowardice in the face of the enemy.'

I thought he was joking until I realized that Hodgson couldn't joke if he tried.

'You'll be needed at the Court Martial as a witness.'

'Oates is one of our best men,' I protested. 'Before he came to us he was with the Third RHA. He's always done a good job with us.

Cowardice sir? Are you sure? What on earth did he do?'

'You know how important it was to lay those telephone lines, we came under fire and Oates did a bunk. It's as simple as that!'

I remembered how silent Oates had been lately and I told the Lieutenant that I had thought the man was sick. We'd had had a bit of a pasting and it was probably a touch of shellshock.

'Nonsense. Oates was perfectly alright. He started to run that line out and when a machine gun got on to us he dropped everything and hid beneath the truck. If that's shellshock we'd all be in the loony bin. No, it was sheer funk. Something we all have to conquer. In the end I had to finish the job myself.'

'Have you sent a report in yet sir?'

I felt my stomach begin to turn. If Oates were to be put on trial his past record would be investigated and everything would come out – how I had deliberately failed to deliver him to that prison camp, how, in fact, I had aided and abetted Oates, a deserter, and then had him put on to the strength of our unit. Oates might be facing a serious charge but I would be lucky if I got away with ten years.

'I sent my report about Oates in to Regiment yesterday.'

If you don't like a man it often follows that he doesn't like you either. Hodgson could see the dismay in my face. He could tell that I wanted him to drop the charges against Oates who was, after all, one of my own crew, but if he knew the real reason my feet wouldn't touch the ground.

'You can forget it,' he said, reading my thoughts, 'Oates is for the high jump and there's nothing you can do about it. Step out of line on this Johnstone and I'll break you?'

After I left Hodgson I did some pretty hard thinking. I determined to try and see the Colonel myself. I would plead with him that Oates was a sick man. I had to get Oates off this dreadful charge not only because I knew that he was no coward but also for my own state of health. It would not be easy to see the Colonel. Normally, one had to apply through the proper channels, in this case Hodgson, and I knew that he would never grant me an interview. I decided, therefore, to see the Colonel myself. The worst they could do would be to put me on a charge but up here in the front line I might even get away with it. Anyway I had a good record and I thought it would be worth chancing and if the report had gone in a day before I would be courting disaster to leave it any longer.

I had never told anyone, even my closest friends, how I had rescued Oates from the military prison and had him put on our strength. Only the RASC man knew about that and he had disappeared for good. I told my crew what Hodgson was doing though, and that Oates was being held on a charge of cowardice and I explained that I was going to see the Colonel to try and get him shipped out as a casualty. They had all got to know Oates pretty well and they all agreed that, although he was a quiet type, he had never shown any sign of breaking before.

'Only that bastard Hodgson would do a thing like this, Corbett exclaimed.

'We're right behind you Sarge,' McAlister said. 'We'll all be witnesses that Oates was a good man to have with us in actionI'

This of course was great news. What better testimony than from his own gun detachment. I drank some black coffee, put Buckley in charge, and went off to see the Colonel. It was a long walk past the other gun positions and then through the conglomeration of transport which clutters up a regimental headquarters but in the end I found the Colonel poring over a map which was spread out on the bonnet of his car. The Sergeant Major and Tubby Wilson were also there. I marched straight up to them and saluted.

'Permission to speak to the Colonel, sir, on an urgent matter!'

The Sergeant Major frowned and drew himself up.

'What's wrong with you Johnstone. You know perfectly well that if you want to see the Colonel you should go through the proper channels!'

But the Colonel was all powerful and he happened to be in a good mood.

'That's alright Sergeant Major. We'll drop the formalities up here. The Sergeant says it's urgent so let him fire away!'

'Sir, it's about Gunner Oates, one of my men. I understand that he is being held in the guardhouse on a charge of cowardice...'

The Colonel shifted uncomfortably and Tubby Wilson stood looking down at his boots.

'Yes, yes, well what about it?'

The Colonel had been trying to thrust this unpleasant business out of his mind. Once in a blue moon, he had told himself, a coward would turn up somewhere. Damn bad luck that it had to be in his regiment! He peered more closely at the map and he was silent for a long time.

'Lieutenant Hodgson has sent in his report and Gunner Oates will stand trial at a Field General Court Martial which will no doubt be held when things quieten down a little up here.'

The Sergeant Major looked at me as if to say 'Right, now clear off while you've got the chance!'

'Gunner Oates is not a coward, sir. He has been a member of my gun team right through this latest battle and he has done his job well. As you know sir we have often been under heavy fire.'

The Colonel went on looking at the map. He then drew a pad towards him and jotted down some notes. Finally he looked up at me impatiently.

'Listen Johnstone. A man may carry on perfectly well under fire and he may even show bravery but that does not mean that one day he will not commit what, in the eyes of others, is an act of cowardice. It's the same thing with a criminal. A man may be perfectly honest all his life and then commit a crime. Now about your man Oates, we lost some of our signallers and Lieutenant Hodgson borrowed Oates from you to help run out a telephone line from the OP to the guns. That job was vital. Setting up that OP was our only chance of finding and destroying those enemy tanks.

Lieutanant Hodgson and Oates came under fire and the line was cut. Oates ran away and the Lieutenant had to mend the line and finish the job himself. By the time he got some bearings down to the guns those tanks were practically out of range. Look here, I detest the stain all this will have on the Regiment but I have no alternative but to act on Lieutenant Hodgson's report.'

'Oates broke down under stress sir. It was shellshock. All my men will testify that he did his job well since this Alamein business started.'

'They may be called as witnesses at the Court Martial. At any rate you certainly will be, Sergeant. We will put down everything you have said and get you to sign a statement in his defence. Incidently, how did Oates come to be posted to our lot in the first place? Where did he come from? Which unit?'

Red warning lights flashed through my brain and my heart began to thump. I knew, then, what it felt like to tug at the ripcord of your reserve parachute.

'His previous unit was smashed up at Alam Halfa sir. He was an experienced gunner and we were short of men so we took him on. It was one of those emergency postings.'

'Which was his unit?' 'The Third RHA, sir.'

'Really? They were a pretty good lot. There can't be much wrong with him if the Third RHA took him on!'

The Colonel told me to wait there while he sent for Lieutenant Hodgson. I would sooner have waited in a minefield. When Hodgson arrived he knew what I was up to immediately and I could tell that he was furious. The Colonel explained that I wanted to assist Oates, a member of my own gun team, who until now had always conducted himself properly whenever we were in action.

'Look here Hodgson, are you determined to go ahead with this? We're busy enough as it is without having to mess about with a Court Martial!'

Hodgson, grim faced, was adamant. 'Oates ran away under fire sir. If everybody did that we might as well pack it in. In my opinion we should set an example to the men. Yes sir, I should like the charge to stand!'

The Colonel looked round at the others helplessly and I could tell that he would seize on any chance to drop the whole business. I played the only card I had.

'If I may make a suggestion sir, there is a course you could take whereby this whole matter would be quickly forgotten with no stain on the honour of the Regiment.'

Hodgson stepped forward angrily but the Colonel waved him back.

'Come on then what is it? What's on your mind?' He looked at his watch impatiently. 'It's time we got on with the war.'

'Send Oates to the MO, sir. Tell him you believe that it's a case of shellshock. Tell him to have him looked at by a psychiatrist!'

The Colonel hesitated, then he opened his briefcase and pulled out the typewritten document which was Hodgson's report on Gunner Oates. Suddenly to our surprise he tore it into shreds.

'Sergeant Major, see that Oates is released from detention and see that he reports to the MO.'

Lieutenant Hodgson, his face red, started to protest but the Colonel silenced him.

'The man cracked up and it is obviously a case for the MO. That's my final word on the matter!'

The Colonel scribbled a note and handed it to the Sergeant Major.

'Here, give the MO this note. Oates is to be treated as a case of shellshock!'

Gosh, it was close. I could almost feel that bonecrushing pull as the white silk billowed above me! I could tell that the Colonel was pleased, too, and greatly relieved that he had found a way of upholding the honour of his Regiment.

Oates disappeared for a while. He probably ended up in a hospital in Cairo – maybe the same one that his girlfriend was working at. Anyway, like water which finds its own level the army clerical system ground its way out and Oates was eventually posted back to us. I refused to have him back on the gun. With the sort of life we were leading I just couldn't take any chances. He could type so he was given a job in the Regimental Headquarters office.

One day we came up against a last-ditch rearguard of Panzer Grenadiers. They were well dug in and supported by a Mark IV tank which straddled the road and blasted everything in sight. We were all packed up, with hatches battened down as it were and with orders to keep up with our forward troops. We could by-pass those Germans easily enough but they would sit there, then, and wreak havoc on the transport coming up behind us. Tubby Wilson ordered us to halt and wait out of range for further instructions. We had just got a nice brew up going when we heard the clatter of a machine gun and the sharp crack of exploding grenades. Another longer burst of machine-gun fire was followed by a violent explosion and black smoke billowed up across the roadblock. We naturally assumed that some of our infantry had stormed the position and destroyed the tank.

We were ordered forward again and as we drove through that scorched and smoking strip of earth we were surprised to see the wreckage of one of our own Regimental Headquarter trucks. Farther on, among the German dead, lay the driver who had been riddled with bullets. The tank was an inferno, the ammunition inside exploding with a fearful racket. We gave it a wide berth as we drove past.

We headed west into the great clouds of dust which rose from the retreating Axis army. The destruction of that roadblock had been just a minor action on the long slog forward, but we wondered about that truck and who it was that had got himself into such a mess back there, and it was Tubby Wilson who told us, later, what had happened.

It was our old friend Oates. He had apparently gone berserk, climbed into the office truck and driven right up close to that enemy position. When his tyres had been shot away and the petrol tank had gone up he had jumped out and charged the Germans with a Tommy gun and a sack of grenades. By some miracle he reached their bunkers and silenced them. Then he pulled the pin out of one of the grenades and swung the whole sack under the belly of the tank. The blast blew that tank wide open. It blew Oates's head off too. A few weeks later we paraded in front of the Colonel who told everybody what had happened back at that road block. Gunner Oates, he informed us, was to be remembered in the future as a hero.

We had been heading west, past all those old battlefields – Mersah Matruh, Hellfire Pass, Tobruk – pushing the Panzerarmee right back to where they had started. We were close to Benghazi and had gone into action alongside some houses which had once belonged to Italian settlers and everytime our gun fired the tiles and pieces of debris came down with a crash. In twenty-four hours those houses had been completely demolished. It was a dark, rainy, miserable day and I think we all had a premonition about the place. Somehow, we had the feeling that this was where we would become unstuck.

The Germans had brought a crack paratroop regiment over from Crete to try and stop our advance. A few days later they went over to the offensive and we were shelled by 88s. It was during the evening and I waited listening for the next shell. We had had orders to take post and we couldn't just run off the gun and take cover.

Crash! We hadn't even heard it coming. Corbett and Shipley received the full blast and were blown to pieces. Nobody could tell which was which when they tried to recover their identity discs. I was sad, especially about Corbett because we had seen a lot of desert together. I knew, too, that I would have to write to their wives. I would sooner have chanced my luck with a dozen 88s.

All I had was a splinter in my leg. One small splinter out of all that steel. Well, that's the way it goes! I spent a couple of weeks in hospital in Cairo. The same hospital that Mary-Anne had once worked in.

They fought the rest of that desert war without me. When I came out of hospital I learned that my regiment had been over-run by tanks and had virtually ceased to exist and, after a spell at Almaza, the Royal Artillery base camp near Cairo, I was posted to another field artillery unit.

Rommel never did keep his dinner appointment at Shepheards. The Panzerarmee was finished. Countless guns, tanks and planes had been destroyed. All the tremendous effort, all the arms and equipment which they had poured into North Africa had come to nothing. There was a time when Rommel could have won hands down, but the arms and petrol he needed so badly were sent to their armies in Russia instead.

Like the Khamseen, that desert wind which blows everything before it, the Eighth Army pushed the Axis armies right out of Africa. Thousands upon thousands of lives had been lost but the desert can soak up a lot of blood and, so they say, the sand is stained red to this day.

After a period of intensive training on new equipment we became part of the 6th Armoured Division whose Divisional sign was a mailed fist, and we soon found ourselves up against a different and a more ferocious German army in the long bloody slog through Italy. My luck held even at Cassino. McAlister survived the war. Buckley, too, who decided to have a go at living in England.

And Mary-Anne? I was always sad that I'd lost her address. That scrap of paper is probably still blowing about in the North African desert. Yes, I did see her again. It was a couple of years after the war. I had kept in touch with Buckley after we had been demobbed but eventually the English climate got him down and he decided to go back to Australia. One day I went down with him to Southampton to see him off on a ship which was packed with homeward-bound Australians. You know what it was like. The crowds, the streamers and confetti, the band playing, the cast – off lines splashing into the water, the ship beginning to move out…

And then I forgot about Buckley because I saw Mary-Anne up there. I tried to convince myself that I was wrong but when I looked again there she was, standing by the rail with a group of Australian girls, and she looked as lovely as ever. She was really quite close, only the gap between us was getting wider all the time. I suddenly wanted to grab one of those lines and pull that ship back into port!

Mary-Anne saw me then, too, and she called out to me but the ship's siren drowned her voice. I waved and called back to her but it was no use. The band had struck up 'Old Lang Syne' and she couldn't hear me. I don't think the old knife has twisted quite so much inside me and as I watched that ship move out my life blood seemed to go with it. The big ship began to swing round until we had just one moment left. I wanted to grab that moment and keep it forever. I wanted to remember how she stood there, slender and like a dream, the light in her auburn hair. I wanted to see her smile again, even if it was through tears, and more than anything else I wanted to tell her how much I loved her.